Christian Education for the African American Community

Teacher Training in the Black Church

Keith A. Chism

Discipleship Resources
Materials for Growth in Christian Faith & Life
Nashville, Tennessee
P.O. Box 840 • Nashville, TN 37202 • Phone (615) 340-7068

Unless otherwise indicated, all scripture quotations are taken from the New Revised Standard Version of the Holy Bible.

ISBN 0-88177-147-3

Library of Congress Catalog Card No. 95-78963

 For information address Discipleship Resources, P. O. Box 840, Nashville, TN 37202-0840. Phone: (615) 340-7068. Fax: (615) 340-7006.

DR147

Contents

Foreword

The black church has long been known for the freedom and exuberance of its worship services. Spirited singing, vibrant preaching, and congregational response are not only expected, they are encouraged. When these important worship forms are experienced at their best, they are powerful forces for spiritual nurture and continuing evangelism. The teaching function of the black church is far behind these more obvious expressions of the faith. That is why it is so important to have a book such as Keith Chism has given to the ecumenical community of faith. Teachers must be trained to share knowledge of the faith in constant and meaningful ways. Learners must learn the faith and have it clearly in mind as the foundation for vital worship.

Dr. Chism writes from a background of one who has lived and worked both in the local church and in the academic community. This book will be helpful to a wide range of persons in the black church but especially to pastors, teachers, and learners of all ages.

James S. Thomas, Ph.D.
Bishop in Residence at Emory University
Candler School of Theology
Atlanta, Georgia

Preface

Education is devalued today, both in the church and in society. Public schools struggle and often fail to pass levies that would secure adequate funds for teaching children and youth. At issue in many teacher strikes is the teachers' perception of a general lack of financial, political, and social support from their community. Buy-outs of teachers' contracts to reduce the cost of salaries of teachers with years of experience override concerns about what experienced teachers bring to the tasks of teaching and learning. In the church the reduction of monetary support is followed, frequently, by a reduction in educational staff and resources. There is a decline in teachers, students, classes, and the production and sale of educational resources. Members are not prepared or willing to teach. Interest in learning continues to dwindle. Congregations are unwilling and/or unready to prepare persons to transmit the knowledge and experiences of Christian faith and guide learners in making sense of life from a Christian point of view. Seldom, in any area of life, does one find persons who are both willing and prepared to adequately address the challenges of the day. And yet, too seldom are investments made, particularly in the church, in the development and nurture of persons in ways that enable the willing to be prepared and challenge the able to be willing.

Keith A. Chism is willing and able. Dr. Chism in his pastorate and through his labor in one such congregation and community, moved from an acceptance of **what is** to a **what if** mode of response. Rather than becoming overwhelmed with members who were willing but unable, he toiled, taught, and nurtured volunteers so they might recognize their experience with God as revealed in the life, death, and resurrection of Jesus of Nazareth; and in knowing, share the blessings of their awareness with others. From his dialectical encounter with these teachers emerges this manuscript that brings together the theory of educational leaders with the practice of God's people.

Dr. Chism uses his personal experience of God, Jesus Christ, and ministry in the church and the experiences of one congregation as the foundation for this work. Thus, the book resonates with questions, concerns, and conversation from his daily walk with a particular people of God in a specific place and moment in history. Yet the insights and wisdom of both the author and the people extend beyond the particularity of their situation. Indeed, **Christian Education for the African American Community** can and will help other pastors, teachers, and congregations prepare those who would be teachers and guides and mentors in the church of Jesus Christ toward a more faithful and fruitful ministry.

In the text, Reverend Chism contends that an increase in the valuation of learning and teaching in the church will coincide with an increase in the preparation of those who teach and lead. Chism cites the critical role and responsibility pastors have for preparing and training persons to transmit the heritage of Christian faith to teachers that they might choose for themselves as well as guide learners in making the Christian heritage their own. He explains the significant benefit to the teacher/servant of understanding and carrying out the teaching office. Chism argues that the purpose of teacher training and development is to nurture teachers to teach, strengthening their skills and confidence in their God-given talents so that their skills and abilities may liberate and lead them—and their learners—to trust in and walk with God. Chism writes in a manner that the words on the pages that follow may be read, studied, and applied in a fashion that the teacher who taught women and children, fishermen and farmers, the poor and the privileged by the Sea of Galilee, might teach us, too.

Joseph V. Crockett
Assistant Professor of Religious Education and Black Church Studies
Colgate-Rochester Divinity School
Bexley Hall
Crozer Theological Seminary

Acknowledgments

No undertaking of this magnitude is possible without the support and affirmation of many special people. I wish to thank the following persons who delicately balanced the criticism and encouragement which helped enhance the quality of this book: Bishop James S. Thomas, Bishop-in-Residence at Emory University, Candler School of Theology, for your guidance and encouragement and mentoring; Dr. Mary Olson, Director of Distance Education at United Theological Seminary, Dayton, for your continuous support throughout my spiritual and academic journey; Dr. Kenneth Ehrman and Dr. Sally Dyck for your editorial suggestions and invaluable assistance; the Reverend Joseph V. Crockett, Assistant Professor of Religious Education and Black Church Studies at Colgate Rochester Divinity School, who is a cherished friend and colleague; Dr. Anne E. Wimberly, for your helpfulness in the refining of the evaluative tools that appear in this book; the Reverend H. Walter Willis, Jr., the former Senior Pastor of Aldersgate United Methodist Church, Warrensville Heights, Ohio, for his wealth of knowledge as an experienced practitioner of Christian education; Jocelyn Roper, for opportunities provided and doors opened; and Carol Lehman, for typing both the original and edited documents.

The majority of this work's contents is the result of the sacrifice, commitment, and vision of the church school teachers I experienced in my ministry at Centenary United Methodist Church, Youngstown, Ohio. You were faithful in attending weekly training sessions; but more important, you have been faithful in teaching God's Word to those who are numbered among the community of faith.

I would also like to thank Dr. William H. Myers, Director of the McCreary Center for African American Religious Studies, Cleveland, Ohio, and the students of the Black Church Studies Program at Ashland Theological Seminary for their words of encouragement and continuous affirmation.

I am deeply indebted to four persons from the General Board of Discipleship: Craig Gallaway for continued encouragement and editorial assistance; Vance P. Ross and Donna Gaither for creative suggestions and constructive criticisms that have strengthened this document. I would also like to thank J. Lee Bonnet for the final editing of this resource.

I am grateful for the love and prayers of three of my dearest and most cherished friends, the Reverends Gilbert T. Davenport, Benita Rollins, and Dennis A. Robinson. Only God knows how important your friendships are to me.

This book is dedicated to Margaret, my wife, Lyndsey Taylor, our daughter, and to my parents, the Reverend and Mrs. L. C. Chism. I hope that this work will be a tangible representation of all the sacrifice that you have made to support me until its completion. Your love and understanding, which are ever so consistent, mean the world to me!

Keith A. Chism
Fall 1995

CHAPTER 1

DEVELOPING A MODEL FOR TEACHER TRAINING: AN OVERVIEW

As a United Methodist pastor of a black congregation, I believe the church school teacher has the ability either to strengthen or to weaken the overall effectiveness of the church school.

Warren J. Hartman speaks of the positive and negative effects of the church school teacher. According to laypersons, pastors, district superintendents, and conference directors, better trained teachers are needed. Furthermore, these persons say the effectiveness and growth of the church school depend on well-trained, dedicated, capable teachers.

These observers also indicate that the decline of the church school may have its roots in the performance of the church school teacher. In most cases, loss of interest, church school dropout, and the decline of the church school all result from poor teaching.[1]

I believe the teaching/learning model proposed here can address the problem of the declining church school. This book offers a teaching/learning alternative that proved helpful in my ministry. Let us explore together the development of a model for teacher training.

THE IMPORTANCE OF PASTORAL LEADERSHIP IN CHRISTIAN EDUCATION

The pastor who wants spiritual growth for the congregation must recognize the importance of Christian education. Floyd Massey, Jr. and Samuel B. McKinney state that the pastor should dream of growing persons rather than of power. They believe an atmosphere must be created where dreaming occurs and where people can take part in the vision. While it has been the practice of most adherents within the black church to judge a pastor according to his or her preaching abilities, true church growth must come from a sound program of Christian education.[2]

The emphasis not only on preaching but also on fund-raising has been detrimental to Christian education, according to Willard A. Williams. He asserts that many churches view Christian education as being only for the children on Sunday morning. He further notes that only a minimal number of black churches can afford to hire a director of Christian education. This leaves the work to volunteers who do their best under difficult circumstances. Williams concludes his argument by saying that Christian education in the black church is weak and must be strengthened. Young persons in The United Methodist Church are complaining; many are leaving our churches because of this weakness. Williams says the answer is not to alter the present emphasis on preaching but to upgrade Christian education through a concerted effort to develop a strong, dedicated leadership program.[3]

This leadership development must start with the pastor. The pastoral leadership must make two determinations regarding the development of a model for teacher training: (1) determine the appropriate teaching/learning strategy and (2) determine the appropriate teacher training model.

To do his or her best to guide the church school in its task of teaching and learning, the pastor must be aware of the needs of persons looking to the church school for ministry. The following is the approach to needs assessment I used in my ministry.

DETERMINING THE APPROPRIATE TEACHING/LEARNING STRATEGY

Needs assessment is paramount. If the church school is to develop an effective teacher training program, it must assess needs accurately.

We attempted to determine whether andragogy or pedagogy was the best teaching/learning model for use within this setting.

Why andragogy or pedagogy? We have viewed religious education from a narrow perspective, emphasizing the acquisition of large bodies of truth while de-emphasizing maturation. The thought of James J. Deboy, Jr. proves applicable here:

> *Education is often seen as the acquisition of knowledge and skills. This is part of education, but the major thrust of education is to enable one to reach full potential as a person in relationship with other persons. Education is not something that is poured into someone from the outside. It is also an internal process which can be facilitated or hindered by outside influences and structures. Education is an orderly and systematic approach to facilitate a person's growth toward maturity.*[4]

A model for teacher training must take into consideration whether one or a combination of both teaching/learning strategies is the most appropriate model. The most accurate means of making this determination is to design a survey. Appendix A, page 59, is a survey that can be used to help with assessment.

The most important issue, however, is the content and subject matter the survey addresses. We must understand the differences between pedagogy and andragogy. The next section of this chapter compares the two.

WHAT ARE PEDAGOGY AND ANDRAGOGY?

The word *pedagogy* is a term derived from the Greek words *paid* (meaning "child") and *agogous* (meaning "leading"). Pedagogy means, literally, the art and science of teaching children.[5] Pedagogy evolved in the monastic schools of Europe between the seventh and twelfth centuries and came to dominate secular schools during their organization in the twelfth century. Learning theory was initially based on the observations of the monks as they taught young children relatively simple skills—reading and writing.

With the advent of elementary schools throughout Europe and North America and their spread through the work of missionaries during the eighteenth and nineteenth centuries, the pedagogical model was accepted. When educational psychologists began to study learning scientifically around the beginning of the twentieth century, pedagogy was further enthroned. The serious study of learning (as opposed to the study of reactions to teaching) did not appear until after World War II.

It wasn't until the 1920s that adult education was organized systematically. Teachers of adults began to experience difficulty with the use of the pedagogical teaching/learning model. The major problem was its very premise: that the purpose of education was the transmittal of knowledge and skills. This age-old purpose suddenly seemed insufficient to adult learners. Not surprisingly, adult educators found adult learners resistant to the strategies prescribed by pedagogy: fact-laden lectures, drill, quizzes, reading assignments, rote memorizing, examinations, etc.[6]

The word *andragogy* is based on the Greek word *aner* (with the stem *andr-*) and means "man, not boy" or adult. Malcolm Knowles originally defined andragogy as the art and science of helping adults learn. Knowles reports that increasing numbers of teachers in elementary and secondary schools (and a few in colleges) are experimenting with the concepts of andragogy because andragogy represents another model of assumptions about learners that can be used alongside pedagogical assumptions.[7]

It is helpful here to compare the two learning models. A pedagogical approach to learning places the learner in a *dependent role:* The teacher is expected by society to take full responsibility for determining what is to be learned, when it is to be learned, how it is to be learned, and if it has been learned. An andragogical approach to learning attempts to move students from dependence toward increasing *self-directedness* but at different rates for different people and in different stages of life. In the andragogical approach, the teacher is responsible for encouraging and nurturing this movement toward self-directedness.[8]

I would cite several other areas to achieve a clearcut comparison between pedagogical and andragogical approaches.

Concept of the learner — A pedagogical approach views the learner as a dependent personality; an andragogical approach views the learner as one who is increasingly self-directed.

Role of learner's experience — A pedagogical approach views the learner's experience as something to be built on; an andragogical approach views the learner's experience as a rich resource for learning.

Readiness to learn — A pedagogical approach says that the learner's readiness to learn varies according to the level of maturation; an andragogical approach asserts that the learner's readiness to learn develops from life tasks and problems.

Orientation to learning — A pedagogical approach says that the learner's orientation to learning is subject-centered; an andragogical approach asserts that the learner's orientation to learning is task- or problem-centered.

Motivation — A pedagogical approach assumes that motivation is derived from external rewards and punishments; an andragogical approach asserts that motivation for learning is derived from internal incentives and curiosity.[9]

Finally, it is necessary to compare the various elements:

Climate — A pedagogical approach to learning tends to have a formal, authority-oriented, competitive, judgmental atmosphere; an andragogical approach to learning encourages a climate that is informal, mutually respectful, consensual, collaborative, and supportive.

Planning — A pedagogical approach to learning places the responsibility for planning in the teacher's hands; an andragogical approach to learning allows both students and teachers to participate in decision-making.

Diagnosis of needs — A pedagogical approach to learning makes the teacher responsible for determining the students' needs; an andragogical approach calls for shared teacher and student assessment of needs.

Setting goals — A pedagogical approach to learning makes the teacher responsible for setting goals; an andragogical approach encourages negotiation between teacher and student for the setting of goals.

Designing a learning plan — A pedagogical approach to learning contains units and course syllabuses, and it follows a logical sequence; an andragogical approach to learning makes use of learning projects and learning contracts, and it follows a sequence defined by the learner's readiness.

Learning activities — A pedagogical approach to learning transmits learning and assigns readings; an andragogical approach to learning uses inquiry projects, independent study, and experiential techniques.

Evaluation — A pedagogical approach to learning places the responsibility for evaluation upon the teacher; an andragogical approach to learning allows for evaluation to be done by mutual assessment.[10]

The comparison of pedagogy and andragogy is helpful as one seeks to determine the appropriate teaching/learning strategy. This approach helps the pastor and church school teachers design an appropriate plan for teaching and learning that will meet the needs of the congregation.

THE IMPORTANCE OF TEACHER TRAINING

Why is teacher training such an important component of the whole Christian education enterprise? It is my contention that this is the foundation upon which a viable Christian education program is built.

As noted earlier, one of the greatest needs within the black church school is a continuous program of teacher training and enrichment. As teachers make a serious effort to enhance their skills, more creativity will arise, and this will become apparent in the form of strengthened classroom performance. Classroom performance is the quality and depth of the classroom teaching presentation. Desirable classroom performance should exhibit thoughtful study of the scriptures, as well as a creative means of transmitting this knowledge to the learner. It also includes the use of a wide range of teaching/learning approaches (audiovisual, participatory, etc.). The primary goal of all teaching in the church school context is transformation. All teachers must understand the connection between classroom performance and transformation in the life of the learner. Every aspect of the classroom teaching presentation should be aimed at transforming the life of the learners and helping them be effective disciples. The desired end, therefore, is that learners will grow in faith toward effective discipleship.

Robert Ulich suggests that too much dependence has been placed on church school guides and manuals; extreme dependence on these aids hampers the creativity of the church school teacher:

> *Unfortunately, too many of the guides and manuals for the Sunday school teachers make a pedantic impression. Even though the majority of these teachers are laymen, must they really be exposed to dozens of course outlines, materials, suggestions as to the beginning, the middle, and the end of a course, recommendations about grouping the children and about handling audiovisual aids, appendices, and bibliographies? All these mental crutches may cripple the teacher's enthusiasm, just as the pedagogy of the old seminaries and normal schools frightened many a young talent away from the teaching profession.*[11]

Our teacher training programs should be of such depth that teachers will not feel bound to the various church school commentaries and aids. We must train our teachers to trust their own God-given gift of teaching and creativity. Myrtle Felkner offers several helpful suggestions for making teacher training programs successful:

> *First, [teaching] must offer spiritual food in terms of (1) warm and loving acceptance of persons just as they are; (2) a common offering of praise, joy, and commitment to the Christ we serve; (3) an affirmation of our task in ways that touch heart and emotion. Motivation to teach the faith hardly ever springs from the intellect. It is nurtured rather by feelings and emotions that claim us and direct us to this particular expression of our discipleship. Second, it must be based on firm, theological, biblical, and educational foundations. Teachers go home to their classrooms with (1) usable and practical methods and skills; (2) a clearer perspective on the importance and purpose of Christian education; (3) a positive feeling about their role as teachers and the teaching ministry of the church, from the biblical dimension.*[12]

Finally, teacher training is evaluated. If teacher training sessions are to be helpful, a means of evaluating these sessions must be developed. Within my ministry, a team of laypersons designed an evaluation process and attended several teacher training sessions. They assessed my effectiveness in addressing the eight areas covered in the sessions.

The teacher's classroom performance should also be evaluated. In my experience it was necessary for the team of laypersons to design an evaluative process and attend various church school classes. By observing the teaching abilities of all the church school teachers, the team was able to identify strengths as well as areas where improvement was needed. Both the teacher training session and classroom evaluation forms appear in Appendix B, page 69.

The use of a collegial approach to the development of an evaluative system proved to be helpful in several ways: (1) It proved to be helpful to me as a facilitator (and strengthened my teaching skills). (2) It helped me identify areas that needed to be addressed in the teacher training sessions. (3) It helped my church develop a concerned, committed group of persons in the ministry of Christian education. (4) It helped pastor and people understand congregational needs in the area of Christian education.

CONCLUSION

This is the foundation upon which this model for teacher training was developed.

Each chapter of this book is designed to offer a theoretical foundation and a teaching/learning strategy for each of the eight topics considered. The end result, I hope, will be a theoretically sound work that is also practical and usable.

A final word: The approach used here was helpful and applicable in my ministry. I offer this approach because I believe that it can be useful to your church; you should, however, be open to adapting this model for your setting. Please use this approach with an open mind and an open heart!

CHAPTER 2

BIBLICAL FOUNDATIONS FOR TEACHER TRAINING

Consideration of teacher training begins with the Bible. The United Methodist Church has always been committed to biblical foundations in Christian education: "Scripture is the primary source by which our Christian knowing and experience are shaped."[13]

The Bible has been described as a love story between "the Lord of all the universe for all time, and a 'stiff-necked' people in the Middle East."[14] Christian education must help persons enlarge their grasp of this love story through a broader understanding of it and a personal appropriation of it.[15]

Ethel R. Johnson and Charles R. Foster believe that this love story has shaped the lives of black people, both individually and as a group. As black people lived through decades of slavery and segregation, the Bible was often the only book that was readily available. As they considered the ancient stories, their imaginations became engaged in looking for ways its themes might make sense of their plight. They identified with the wilderness experience of the Exodus people and recognized the longing for a promised land in which the "balm of Gilead" would restore wholeness to daily living. In short, they embraced the biblical narrative. Black people have experienced the presence of the risen Savior and entered into the biblical experience "incarnationally," claiming it as their story.[16]

My proposed model for teacher training acknowledges that black United Methodists experience education in a complex context. While we retain a religious experience that is uniquely our own, we exist in the midst of a predominately white denomination. While our church is made up of various nationalities and races, we share a common faith that binds all Christians. We all celebrate a pilgrimage that finds expression in various ways. Worship styles may vary, and the means by which faith is taught to new generations could well be different too.[17]

The distinct pilgrimage of black Americans must be understood through the biblical narrative. Church school teachers must relate the word of God to the religious, social, economic, and personal facets of the black experience. Just as our ancestors found an analogy with the Old Testament nation of Israel, the modern-day black Christian must see the connections between the scriptures and today's pilgrimage. As Johnson, Shockley, and Foster have said: "The everyday poignancy and pain of the black experience provides, in other words, a window on the biblical experience that was not shared by the majority white population."[18] Christian educators in the black church must teach the meaning of the biblical narrative from our unique black perspective.[19]

To begin to do so, the church school teacher should understand the biblical origins of Christian education in the Old and New Testaments.

EDUCATION DURING OLD TESTAMENT TIMES

The center of education in the faith is the "Shema" passage found in Deuteronomy 6:4-9. This passage is more a part of the Jewish consciousness than any document and has become ingrained in the mind of Gentile people.[20] Consider these words:

> *Hear, O Israel: The Lord is our God, the Lord alone. You shall love the Lord your God with all your heart, and with all your soul, and with all your might. Keep these words that I am commanding you today in your heart. Recite them to your children and talk about them when you are at home and when you are away, when you lie down and when you rise. Bind them as a sign on your hand, fix them as an emblem on your forehead, and write them on the doorposts of your house and on your gates.*

> *Education in the Old Testament took place in the midst of life. The teachers were parents, prophets, priests, sages, and poets.[21] Education was not segregated from other aspects of life; it was so intricately interwoven with life that if one failed in teaching and learning, he or she failed at life itself.[22]*

Parents' teaching served as the foundation of faith for the children.[23] Children learned through: (1) participation in informal, everyday activities and special events, such as feasts and fasts; (2) parental control of children's conduct; and (3) the passing down of the oral tradition.[24]

Learning was informal. For example, a mother could teach her children about the sabbath meal as she performed her household duties: preparing the sabbath meal, lighting the sabbath lamp, and performing the sabbath rites.[25]

The father also played a role in the educational process. He taught his children scripture recitation and memorization, and the commands of the Shema. The children were taught about the repulsive nature of sin and the virtues of honesty, industry, sobriety, and obedience. When the son reached the age of personal accountability as defined by the law (bar mitzvah), the father publicly thanked God that he was no longer responsible for his son's actions.[26]

There is a need for this biblical principle to be appropriated to the needs of the African American community, specifically to address the absence of the father in many African American families. Jawanza Kunjufu contends that only men can develop boys into men; such a significant act should not be attempted by a woman alone. Kunjufu notes that, although 62 percent of African American children are raised by single mothers, there are few instances in which families receive no input from a male figure (i.e., grandfather, father, brother, uncle, nephew, cousin, neighbor, lover, or friend). Without a male figure, the family, streets, television, school, and church come up lacking as models. A concerted effort must be made between African

American women and men to actively fill the void. Kunjufu concludes that until African American men become responsible for giving direction to at least one male child, the destruction of black boys will continue.[27]

The black church must teach its men the importance of modeling appropriate lifestyles. Men must be prepared to lead rites-of-passage programs; combat the intrusions of drugs, drug dealers, and gangs; and help black boys resist negative peer pressure. Just as the men of the Old Testament modeled biblical principles, so too should black men lead the children today.

Although the parents provided most religious education for children in the Old Testament period, other persons also made significant contributions. The prophets spoke forth for God; they interpreted the meaning of day-to-day events. They addressed ethical issues by offering spiritual insight and hope to the disinherited, the sincere official, the simple man.[28]

Priests reflected their understanding of the will of God through ritual, altar, and sacrifice. The priest not only offered instruction regarding the temple service but also taught the law itself. Deuteronomy 31:9-13 states that Moses wrote the law and gave it to the sons of Levi. Moses further commanded that it be read to all Israel—men, women, children, and sojourners—so that they might hear the law and fear the Lord. Thus, the priests were the public teachers for the nation of Israel.[29]

Finally, the sages and poets made contributions to the educational process. The sages offered their wisdom, and it was written down and became a rich body of material. This material offered moral guidance to young persons. This wisdom often appeared in poetic form, making it conducive to learning, as in the Book of Proverbs.[30]

The poets contributed to the educational process through their psalms and proverbs. Others participated with them in reading their poetry, sometimes in unison and sometimes antiphonally. Many of these poems were sung and chanted.[31] Some scholars believe that the Old Testament poetry represents the most significant contribution of the Hebrew people to world literature.[32]

For the Old Testament people there was no artificial distinction between theory and practice; they attempted to live out in daily life the commands of God. Robert Ulich offers this comment:

> *In no way were the Jews satisfied with general moral precepts; they had to transfer them into the daily practical life of a nation for whom obedience to the Torah (the Pentateuch or the Law of Moses) was synonymous with the preservation of the Covenant and, consequently, with national survival and salvation.*[33]

For the Jews, therefore, *keeping* the law meant *living* the law.

Education During New Testament Times

The source of education during New Testament times was Jesus Christ himself. In the words of John: "And the Word became flesh and lived among us, and we have seen his glory, the glory as of a father's only son, full of grace and truth" (John 1:14). Christ's disciples accepted the literal meaning of "the Word made Flesh." The crucifixion of Jesus was interpreted as an act of reconciliation between God the judge and man the sinner. The resurrection of Christ and his promised return were seen as victory over death, hell, and the grave.[34]

The disciples accepted the literal meaning of John's words because of the example of Jesus himself. Sid Smith offers the following insight:

> *Jesus was a master incarnational teacher: He was "the Word become flesh" (John 1:14). He was an example of the truth He taught; He was a perfect role model for His lessons. He did not simply tell His disciples how to pray; He showed them. He did not merely articulate what love was like; He demonstrated it. He not only talked about God; He acted like God.*[35]

Jesus knew that, by teaching incarnationally and modeling the truth, ultimately his disciples would take on his likeness.[36] Lee Magness says:

> *One statement of Jesus, almost an understatement, may provide the clearest insight into the purposeful way Jesus taught and the objective he had in mind: "A learner is not superior to the teacher nor is a slave superior to his master. It is sufficient for the learner to become like his teacher, and the slave like his master" (Mt. 10:24-25, par.). Learning was the means of relating to Jesus, but the goal was broader than the assimilation of facts, the adoption of a body of tradition, or even identification with a philosophical position. For the disciples, learning was living, living with and like Jesus. Perhaps, we should interpret more literally: learning was becoming, being like Jesus. Education in Christ was not even merely the mimicry of Jesus' habits; it was growth into a state of being which was Christ-like.*[37]

Education during New Testament times was also dependent upon the Apostle Paul. Charles A. Tidwell says that Paul was second only to Jesus in teaching greatness and offers the following reasons: (1) Paul was educationally advantaged from birth: he was born a Roman citizen in Tarsus. This city had a reputation for scholarship. When Paul was arrested in Jerusalem and told the soldier where he was from, the soldier knew that Paul was a learned man. (2) Paul had a superior education: Acts 22:3 indicates that he sat at the feet of Gamaliel, one of the greatest teachers of his day. (3) Paul was perceived as a teacher: many were not easily convinced of the validity of his apostleship, but none contested his claim that he was a teacher (see Acts 21:28). (4) Paul's teaching was effective: this is clear as he instructed the Church at Antioch (Acts 11:19-26). (5) Paul taught in the synagogues: he would enter communities and go to the synagogues and teach (see Acts 13:14-52 and Acts 17:1-3, 10-12). (6) Paul taught wherever and whomever he could: he taught a variety of people in a variety of places. (7) Paul used various methods to teach: he used discourse and discussion (Acts 13:14-52) as he sought to instruct, correct, and persuade. (8) Paul admonished pastors to teach: he said that a bishop (pastor) "must be . . . an apt teacher" (2 Tim. 3:2). Paul gives Timothy important instruction on the teaching task in 2 Tim. 2:2; 3:16-17, and 4:2. (9) Paul taught faithfully throughout his ministry: he believed in education and advocated it for other persons. Paul modeled his convictions.[38]

It is my conviction that Paul stands as a marvelous model of teaching as it occurred in the New Testament. Paul lived out his faith in the same manner as Jesus.

The Relevance of the Old and New Testaments to the Task of Teacher Training

Modeling was central to Old Testament Christian teaching. Children eventually embraced the faith by seeing it lived out. The church school teacher must model and live out biblical principles if the Bible is to be relevant to persons. This concept of modeling is particularly important within the black community; there is a great need for persons who model Christian behavior and principles. With the prevalence of AIDS, drugs, illiteracy, homelessness, and other pressing social issues, it is essential that biblical principles be made relevant to everyday life.

Modeling is also important because of the rise of divorce and single-parent homes. Many young people in the black community live in environments where the lifestyle is antithetical to Christian living. The church school must present an acceptable alternative. It must participate in parenting from a biblical perspective; it worked in Old Testament times, and it works today.

The New Testament offers another important Christian education concept: incarnational teaching. Sid Smith explains:

> *Incarnational teaching means the lesson is "made flesh" in the lives of the teacher and students. In other words, the goal of this style of teaching is to have the lessons manifested in the lifestyles of both teacher and pupil.*[39]

Jesus offers us an excellent model of incarnational teaching. The Apostle Paul also gives us insight into teaching: he modeled Christian living.

Conclusion

I have attempted to show the need for understanding the biblical foundations of Christian education. Church school teachers need to understand these concepts to serve effectively.

TEACHING/LEARNING STRATEGY

(1) **Read Deuteronomy 6:4-9** — Discuss the relevance of this passage to Christian education.

(2) **Read Proverbs 22:6** — Discuss the relevance of this passage to Christian education. Adherents to the early Jewish faith embraced the principles of the Shema as a way of life. The Jews of old taught the Word of God in the midst of their lives, in everyday settings; the teachings of the Torah were made relevant to real life. "The Word became flesh."

(3) **Read John 1:14** — Discuss the relevance of this passage to Christian education. With such incarnational teaching, the life of a child was shaped for the duration of life's pilgrimage. When God's truth and ways are taught from birth through adulthood, there is a strong possibility that these teachings will manifest themselves in that life.

(4) Discuss ways black Americans have experienced God's Word "incarnationally." Specific examples?

Discuss These Issues:

Question 1: How does this passage speak to the role of the parent in Christian education?

Question 2: As a church school teacher, how can you help to make these three passages relevant to the lives of adults and children?

Learning Activity

1. Gather into groups and discuss specific examples of incarnational teaching in your lives as parents. How have you lived out these passages as parents and grandparents?
2. Ask each teacher to spend a few moments reflecting on this truth: "More teaching is done by example than by precept." Then ask each to list specific steps he or she will take to be a better model for students and others encountered in everyday life.

Wrap-Up

Closing Prayer

Chapter 3

Servanthood as It Relates to Teacher Training

The church of Jesus Christ is threatened anew by materialism in every generation. As we attempt to offer ministry, we are constantly confronted by persons obsessed with material gain. The temptation the church faces is the desire to be materially successful; the call of God, however, is to be *faithful.*

As we attempt to motivate volunteers, we must articulate biblical/ theological principles that put their work into proper perspective. They need a biblical frame of reference to shape their attitudes and perceptions. I propose a focus on servanthood. If church school teachers embrace the Old and New Testament principles of servanthood, the task of teaching will prove to be enriching. Let us consider the Old and New Testament foundations of servanthood.

Old Testament Foundations of Servanthood

In our society, servanthood is not viewed as a position of respect. Our world is characterized by a desire to control and possess, rather than a desire to allow ourselves to be controlled and possessed. We are most willing to have others meet our needs, while in truth we aren't willing to meet the needs of others. So when we speak of worldly servanthood it isn't a very desirable walk of life. If we look at servanthood from a biblical perspective, however, we see that God's Word redefines servanthood, enabling us to see it in a new light.

Lawrence Richards and Clyde Hoeldtke assert two primary meanings for the term *servant.* First of all, the nation of Israel is referred to as a servant nation and its people as God's chosen people. Second, a servant is promised a Deliverer. The important point about being named "servant" is that it connotes that one who is recognized as such is endowed with God's special care and is able to relish the special nature of the relationship with the one to whom one is personally committed.[40] These themes find expression in the words of the prophet Isaiah:

> *But now hear, O Jacob my servant, Israel whom I have chosen! Thus says the Lord who made you, who formed you in the womb and will help you: Do not fear, O Jacob my servant, Jeshurun whom I have chosen.* (Isaiah 44:1-2)

This particular passage portrays Israel as the servant of the Lord:

> *The usual collocation of servant and chosen one (whom I have chosen) appears at the crucial point in the poem. It was through her election that Israel became the servant of the*

> *Lord. Yahweh chose Israel to be his servant. His purpose was to be fulfilled in the servant.*[41]

Servanthood in the Old Testament is not even primarily focused on the nation of Israel. As Old Testament biblical prophecy makes plain, a figure will arise who will be the very embodiment of God and will show us a true picture of what servanthood is. This is borne out in Isaiah 42:1-4:

> *Here is my servant, whom I uphold, my chosen, in whom my soul delights; I have put my spirit upon him; he will bring forth justice to the nations. He will not cry or lift up his voice, or make it heard in the street; a bruised reed he will not break, and a dimly burning wick he will not quench; he will faithfully bring forth justice. He will not grow faint or be crushed until he has established justice in the earth; and the coastlands wait for his teaching.* (Isaiah 42:1-4)

The servant portrayed here will be in possession of God's Spirit. For a servant to fulfill the prophetic task, he or she must be endowed with the Spirit which provides illumination and empowerment. God doesn't assign a duty without providing the necessary equipment. The servant who possesses God's Spirit is a source of delight for the Lord.[42]

Another interesting quality of the servanthood picture as depicted by Isaiah is that the servant is an advocate of justice. The rights and the privileges of the despised, the damned, and the disinherited are the concern of this servant. Though the servant described here will be met with opposition, he continues on and isn't discouraged.[43]

New Testament Foundations of Servanthood

Gilbert A. Peterson states that the New Testament offers three terms that describe leaders. A leader is a **shepherd;** Peter is told to tend or shepherd *(poimaino)* the sheep in John 21:16. A leader is a *kabernesis,* **"administrator"** (the literal meaning is "steering a ship"). First Corinthians 12:28 uses this term to denote administering or caring for details in an orderly manner. Finally, the term found in Luke 22:27 has to do with **servanthood:** servant leadership doesn't lord it over others *(kurieuo)* but serves *(diakanos).*[44]

One of the greatest accomplishments of Jesus' earthly ministry is that he set a new precedent of servanthood. For Jesus, servanthood was linked to greatness. If any person is desirous of attaining true greatness, he or she will do it by being the servant of all. Consider the words of Mark:

> *But it is not so among you; but whoever wishes to become great among you must be your servant, and whoever wishes to be first among you must be slave of all. For the Son of Man came not to be served but to serve, and to give his life a ransom for many.* (Mark 10:43-45)

The idea of servanthood isn't a popular notion in the minds of many. Yet, Jesus tells us that this is the means by which we can attain true greatness. In this particular dialogue, James and John are desirous of having the distinction of sitting on Jesus' right and left hands in glory. In their minds these "high level political positions" represent the ultimate in greatness.

But Jesus asks James and John some very searching and profound questions about their willingness to endure suffering and persecution for the sake of the kingdom. He challenges them instead to be the best servants they can be.

On February 4, 1968, Martin Luther King, Jr. preached a sermon entitled "The Drum Major Instinct" from the pulpit of Ebenezer Baptist Church in Atlanta, Georgia. In his sermon, Dr. King talked about the desire for greatness being a good instinct if we are able to use it correctly. He further exhorted listeners to strive to be first, explaining, however, that the desire to be first and to be great must be understood in light of Jesus' definition of greatness, which is to be a servant.[45] Dr. King helps us understand that everyone is capable of servant ministry.

Lawrence O. Richards cites the Matthew 20:25-28 account of James' and John's misconceptions about leadership. Richards asserts that we see two conflicting models of leadership in this passage. One model, the secular ruler model, portrays leaders as persons who exercise authority over others. While this model is not wrong in itself, it is wrong in the church. The second model, as offered by Jesus, is that of the servant leader. Leaders within the Body of Christ are not *over* us but *among* us; they are not rulers but slaves, givers rather than takers. If the nature and function of leadership in the church are to be fully understood, the servant model, as offered by Jesus, must be taken with complete seriousness.[46]

Richards further discusses the dimensions of servanthood:

(1) **The servant relationship.** The servant leader is the one who is *among*, not *over* those whom he or she leads. Being among means that we perceive other persons as being like ourselves, and that persons enter a relationship of self-revelation and mutual ministry.

(2) **The servant task.** The servant leader who is among fellow disciples follows Jesus' model and expends his or her life on behalf of others.

(3) **The servant method.** While our culture often views leadership as directive, the servant leader is unable to command. Servant leaders do not "lord it over" others; servant leaders *lead by example.* The words of Peter describe how God wants us to serve: "not lord it over those in your charge, but be examples to the flock" (1 Peter 5:1-5).[47]

Everyone can be a servant, because everybody can serve. This has a profound relationship to the task of teaching within the church school.

THE RELATIONSHIP OF BIBLICAL SERVANTHOOD PRINCIPLES TO THE TASK OF TEACHING

There are several reasons for advocating servant ministry.

First, church school teachers must understand that our motivation to give service arises from biblical servanthood principles. It is my belief that if we view the task of teaching and the whole of life as an opportunity to give service, we can accept our calling to teach in its proper perspective.

Second, the church school teacher is unique as a called servant of God. Though church school teachers sense their inadequacies (as all servant leaders do), through proper preparation and the guidance of the Holy Spirit, everyone who is called to teach can serve. The church school teacher accepts his or her role as a called servant of God. In response to the calling, the church school teacher must respond in commitment by properly preparing.

William H. Myers points out that the oral tradition has been evident in the long history of African American churches. Slave narratives, conversion narratives, Negro spirituals, black preaching, and antiphonal call and response are examples. Call narratives represent a significant aspect of this oral tradition, Myers contends. Legitimization, acceptance, authority, and ordination are all dependent upon the oral articulation of a divine call. Even though African American religion has evolved from preliterate to literate, oral articulation still has a place in the community.[48]

I believe the call extends to the work of educational ministry, to those who participate in the ordained ministry and to the laity. Calling is clearly consistent with the spiritual heritage of the black church.

Finally, servant ministry allows the church school teacher to experience rewards not based on material considerations. If a church school teacher sees an observable change in the life of one person as a result of his or her encounter with the Word of God, the teaching task is worthwhile. This is especially important within the black church, because many congregations fail even to recognize those who give faithful service within the church school.

CONCLUSION

I have examined several Old and New Testament passages that focus on servanthood. I hope the information offered will prove helpful in moving church school teachers to embrace the principles of servanthood. I have also attempted to show the relevance of the biblical narrative to the task of church school teaching.

TEACHING/LEARNING STRATEGY

In the Old Testament

(1) Servanthood is a high and special calling that involves a covenantal relationship with God.

(2) Servanthood is not forced obedience to a thoughtless Master; there is a willing commitment by the servant to a Master who is fully committed to the servant as well.

(3) Because of the willing commitment that we make and the covenantal relationship that we enter into with God, we make a free commitment to serve God and the church for life.

In the New Testament

The most important insight into servanthood in the New Testament is contained within the Gospels and modeled by the life and ministry of Jesus. Three key passages show us the manner in which Jesus provided the greatest example of servanthood:

Read each of these passages and identify what you learned about servanthood.

(a) Mark 10:45 (b) Matt. 23:8-12 (c) John 12:12-17

A real-life case study of conflicting models of leadership:

Read Matt. 20:25-28.

What do we learn from Jesus about leadership models?

There are two conflicting models of leadership—the secular ruler model and the servant model.

- The secular ruler model "lords it over them."
- In the servant model, "Greatness is defined not by favoritism, but by fitness."
- The secular ruler model "exercises authority over them."
- In the servant model, "The greatest of all is the slave who serves all at the great banquet."

There is nothing wrong with the secular ruler model of leadership in the world; Jesus is saying that it is wrong *in the kingdom of God.* He says to his disciples, "Not so with you."

Question

As a church school teacher, what are the implications from these two models and how do they relate to your work in the church school?

After discussion of the question, the facilitator may offer these comments in summary fashion:

(1) **The servant relationship.** The servant is a person who is among, not over those whom he or she leads. Persons perceive others to be like themselves, and they freely share in the give-and-take of self-revelation and mutual ministry.

(2) **The servant method.** Leaders in our culture are seen as directive; their task is to tell. But the servant method does not "lord it over" others. The way of the secular ruler is cut off from the church by the words of Jesus: "Not so with you." (Read 1 Peter 5:1-5.)

(3) **The servant task.** The servant must expend his or her life on behalf of others. This may involve service beyond ordinary expectations.

Learning Activity

Make a detailed list of contrasts and comparisons between servant and secular ruler styles. Discuss the list and its relevance to the task of teaching.

Closing Discussion Question

Do you have a servant's attitude and a servant's leadership style? Is it enough to have a "servant's heart"?

Closing Prayer

CHAPTER 4

TEACHING/LEARNING PHILOSOPHY

Our world places a great deal of emphasis on acquiring information. Many of us feel that our society is growing increasingly impersonal, de-emphasizing the human mind and intellect while relying more upon machines and automation. This tendency has far-reaching implications for the church, especially the church school.

I believe the church school must not become so engrossed in the information age that it loses touch with its commitment to the individual. While the tendency has been to equate quality with voluminous information, the church school teacher must emphasize the importance of the individual.

WHAT IS A PREFERRED TEACHING/LEARNING PHILOSOPHY?

In order to be effective, church school teachers must understand the functions of both the teacher and the learner. A philosophy must be established.

John Dewey identified the role of the teacher as a *framer of the learning environment*. The teacher is one who guides and directs the impulses and interests of students to a specific process or task. This process stands in sharp contrast to the concept of the teacher as one who indoctrinates students with a predetermined body of truth. The teacher is, therefore, a *guide* rather than a dispenser of predetermined truth.[49]

Dewey's insight into the learner also proves to be helpful. He believed in freedom for the learner—not uncontrolled freedom, but active participation in planning the learning process.[50]

Although all teachers do not share Dewey's sentiments, I would challenge you to consider its usefulness in this teacher training model.

To begin an evaluation of philosophy, you might ask two questions: (1) What do your church school teachers understand *Christian education* to mean? (2) Do your church school teachers approach the teaching task from a pedagogical or andragogical perspective? Examining these two key issues will prove helpful in developing a model for teacher training.

Malcolm Knowles proved helpful to me when I approached this task. Knowles urges us to reexamine our thinking and our notions about the very purpose of education. Referring to the terminology, "the knowledgeable person," Knowles asserts that we have had the faith that if we pour enough information and knowledge into persons, they will be good people and will know how to use their knowledge wisely. Knowles further states that this faith may have been justified or understandable when it arose in an era of relative stability: knowledge and technology changed gradually and education was thought to be a right and a privilege for the leisured class.[51]

Knowles defines the mission of education in this way:

We now know that in the world of the future we must define the mission of education as to produce competent people—people who are able to apply their knowledge under changing conditions; and we know that the foundational competence all people must have is the competence to engage in lifelong self-directed learning. We now know, also, that the way to produce competent people is to have them acquire their knowledge (and skills, understandings, attitudes, values, and interests) in the context of its application.[52]

Knowles' philosophy also applies to the question of pedagogy/andragogy. He had to redefine his role in the teaching/learning process when he experienced dissonance as he started experimenting with self-directed learning. Knowles had perceived his role as a transmitter of content and judge of the students' mastery of data. Knowles saw his main function as implementing a plan addressing four questions: (1) What content needs to be covered? (2) How can this content be organized into manageable units? (3) How can these units be organized into a logical sequence? (4) What means of transmission will be most efficient for transmitting each unit?

But his self-concept has changed from teacher to facilitator. He had to change focus from what is happening in the student to what the teacher is doing. A change in teaching/learning philosophy of such drastic proportions required self-disclosure; Knowles had to examine his approach—his worries, strengths, weaknesses, hopes, aspirations, insecurities, etc.[53]

While Knowles is probably best known for his contributions to secular education, he offers educational principles applicable to the Christian context. As I examined the needs of my context, I realized it was necessary to start the movement away from transmitting content and toward facilitating learning. We need to help teachers see the validity of making this transition.

A second point made by Knowles centers around the issue of producing competent people. Church school teachers must ultimately ask themselves, Is it more important to offer volumes of information or to help persons reach their fullest Christian potential? While it is extremely important to have a well-prepared presentation, we must see the need to help develop competent Christian persons.

The third point relevant to our discussion has to do with self-disclosure or exposure. When a church school teacher adapts a teaching/learning philosophy such as the one proposed by Knowles, he or she must come to grips with the willingness (or lack thereof) to cease being perceived as an authority figure. This means that teacher and learner view themselves as *partners* in the entire teaching/learning experience; each person brings a uniqueness to the learning experience that is deeply valued. This calls for openness and self-disclosure on the part of both teacher and student.

Other educators contribute to a new philosophy as well. Lowell E. Brown and Bobbie Reed also stress the importance of a teaching/learning philosophy that emphasizes the need for life changes, as opposed to transmitting data and information. Brown and Reed advocate a style of teaching that actively involves the learner:

> *Both secular and Christian educators who have studied the results of different teaching methods are discovering that a learner learns infinitely better when he/she is actively involved in the teaching/learning process, as opposed to when he/she is only passively listening.*[54]

Lawrence O. Richards echoes the validity of this approach. Richards says that church school teachers love, nurture, and build faith community relationships, despite the disadvantages imposed by limited time. The Sunday school (or church school) hour can be a time of significant ministry. Here lives can be touched and transformed. Richards underscores, however, that many Sunday school (or church school) teachers merely transmit data and information.[55]

Linda J. Vogel offers an approach to teaching older adults similar to Knowles'. Knowles views the role of the learner's experience as a rich resource for learning. This viewpoint represents an andragogical approach to learning; the pedagogical approach sees the learner's experience as something to be built upon.[56] Vogel says that, in planning teaching and learning experiences, we must begin with the realm of people's experiences and life journeys. Nothing is more threatening than to encounter something that seems entirely foreign; because older adults have a rich range of life experiences, we must incorporate them into the planning for teaching and learning.[57] According to the 1993 *Foundations*, "Because we take seriously the life-changing nature of Christian education, we will create a community that nurtures faith by emphasizing life experiences as occasions for spiritual insight."[58]

If we expect our students to grasp biblical truths, we must involve them in the teaching/learning process. This brings home the need for individual teacher creativity:

> *To be sure they have actually taught, teachers need to be able to identify observable changes in the lives of the learners as a result of the Bible study which has been provided.*[59]

The fundamental philosophical question is this: Is the student a jug to be filled or a plant to be nurtured?[60]

Formulating a Teaching/Learning Philosophy That Is Compatible with the Black Context

Because this model for teacher training concerns itself with the black context in particular, there are certain aspects that must be considered in formulating a teaching/learning philosophy. Anthony J. Shipley speaks of the distinct nature of Christian education within the black church:

> *Christian education enables each person to experience the reality and love of God and to respond in faith and love. He/she then makes a commitment to God and strives to become fully human as he/she seeks to reach his/her highest potential. Christian education in the black church must create learning environments in which lifestyle and tradition are used as vehicles to communicate the message of Jesus Christ.*[61]

Church school teachers must take into account the particular needs of African American persons. Shipley offers further insight, exploring six areas that should be considered:

1. **Information.** The facts of the Christian faith represent an integral part of the learning environment. For education to be of a Christian nature, the biblical facts about our faith must be included regardless of the style of the teaching/learning experience. It is unwise to substitute process for content: Christian education within the black context must address the content of the faith.

2. **History.** In the black church, black Christian history must be present in the content. Data should be included not only about recent Christian saints such as Martin Luther King, Jr. but also about the Christian saints of slavery, such as Harriet Tubman, Frederick Douglas, Daniel Hale Williams, Benjamin Banneker, and others. Black youth should understand that Christianity was not the sole possession of the white man, but that the Christian faith did, does, and always will belong to black people as well.

3. **Nurture.** God entrusts church school teachers with the sacred task of nurturing persons, through their lifestyles and actions, so that they can be fed and grow. Teachers must be willing to give of themselves—their souls and their bodies—so that others can be developed and nurtured. The task of the enabler is to prepare our own lives in order that we will have something to give.

4. **Economic Insight.** In a capitalistic society such as the United States, it is important for black people to understand the importance and power of mass capital. The future of the race, as well as of our lives and our families, depends upon our capacity to care, save, and use conglomerate sums of money to better the human good of all. We must help black youth understand the value of work and distinguish between work that is clearly exploitation of human labor and work that is valued by our society. Finally, the black church must help black youth understand the value of money as a vehicle for enhancing and broadening their range of choices.

5. **Political Knowledge and Action.** We must teach black youth that politics are power; politics represent a part of the Christian responsibility for minorities if change is going to come.

6. **Purpose and Goal.** United Methodism has always been characterized by ethnic diversity; ethnic churches have served a clear purpose in making Jesus Christ incarnate in a language and style that helped each group to unify its purposes. As groups have unified their purposes, they have moved toward the goal of producing ethnic Christians who make a Christian contribution to American life. Shipley concludes, therefore, that the black church is charged with the responsibility of creating learning environments in a style and language that cause black Christians to come forth able to contribute to American life.[62]

There are other scholars who advocate teaching/learning philosophies that meet the needs of African Americans. Janice E. Hale-Benson contends that in colonialism the domination of a people is as important as their exploitation because domination is the means by which exploitation can be maintained. The educational system, therefore, must foster cultural repression and create a rationale for colonialism. Under a system of colonialism, as Hale-Benson notes, the colonizer has a dual purpose for educating the colonized. First, the socialization process causes the colonized to accept the value system, history, and culture of the dominant society. Second, education is a tool to foster economic productivity. The oppressed are commodities imbued with skills that are bought and sold on the labor market for the profit of the capitalists. The educator who is an advocate for liberation has opposing purposes for educating the oppressed: education for struggle and education for survival.[63]

Education for struggle, according to Hale-Benson, has a consciousness-raising function for black people, and addresses the following realities: (a) who they are; (b) who the enemy is; (c) what the enemy is doing to them; (d) what to struggle for; (e) what form the struggle must take.[64]

This educational approach reverses the effects of "miseducation," as chronicled by Carter G. Woodson. Woodson views miseducation as a process that facilitates intellectual genocide on black people and drains potential leadership from the struggle for liberation. Woodson contends that most black people who have been educated under oppressive educational systems are not equipped to struggle for liberation until they "recover" from their education. They are taught by the oppressor how to function in the best interest of the oppressive system. In this process, the oppressed take on the characteristics of the oppressor.[65] As Paulo Freire notes, education, when viewed as the practice of freedom, clearly denies that humanity is abstract, isolated, independent, and unattached to the world. Education as the practice of freedom also denies that the world exists as a reality apart from humanity. Authentic reflection considers neither abstract humanity nor the world without humanity but humanity in its relation with the world.[66]

Finally, Hale-Benson states that education must also be for survival, as individual survival is tied to the survival and development of black people. Education for survival attempts to reduce individualism and competition. While this model of education is primarily designed for use in public schools, with appropriate contextual modification these suggestions can be successfully adapted for use within the black church. She suggests that the following features should characterize the model:

(1) **High affective support.** Plan classrooms with a high adult-student ratio, small-group learning, and heterogeneous grouping (family style). Encourage frequent touching, lap sitting, holding hands, and hugging.
(2) **Self-concept development.** Enhance children's self-confidence through frequent compliments, praise, display of work, performances, open houses, and success experiences.
(3) **Creative expression.** All types of creative expression should be represented within the curriculum. Encourage the visual, dramatic, and musical arts.
(4) **Arts and crafts.** When working with children, choose forms and themes that emphasize African and African American culture.
(5) **Activities.** Provide frequent activities that allow for physical release and learning through play. An integral part of this area

should be dance and creative movement. Organize the classroom to allow maximum child movement.

(6) **African culture.** Plan for exposure to African culture that is appropriate for various age levels and comprehension—foods, geography, fashions, music, instruments, song, poetry, names, history, and art.

(7) **African American culture.** Emphasize African American culture—foods, music, folklore, art, literature, and history.

(8) **Extracurricular experiences.** Plan frequent educational fieldtrips. Invite a variety of "teachers" from the community—as well as parents and grandparents (elders)—to teach special skills.

(9) **Holidays.** Attention should be given to the politics of holidays, and particularly how they affect the history of African American people and other oppressed people in America. For example, Thanksgiving should not be discussed solely from the point of view of the pilgrims. Make it an exploration of the situation of Native Americans, African Americans, and the European colonizers. Celebrations, and commemorations should focus upon events and historical figures pivotal in the African American liberation struggle.[67]

Hale-Benson also recommends culturally specific teaching strategies which are useful for the educational purposes of the black church:

(1) **Body language.** Black children make use of nonverbal communication. Teachers should exhibit sensitivity to the use of gestures, eye contact, and other nonverbal cues.

(2) **Standard English.** Standard English should be modeled, and children's speech should be informally corrected. This is important in early childhood, as children need to develop the ability to "hear" certain sounds and to reproduce them early in life. Teachers should also speak in complete sentences and encourage the children to do so.

(3) **Equal talking time.** Teacher "talk" should be regulated to the approximate amount of child talk. The teacher should encourage the children to talk conversationally, in recitation, and creatively.

(4) **Group learning.** An emphasis should be placed on small group learning and hands-on contact with the teacher. When children are not working with adults, they should be learning with peers.

(5) **A variety of learning activities.** Children should be taught using various learning activities—movement, games, music, prose, poetry.

(6) **Music in the classroom.** Afro-American music should permeate the curriculum. The children should be exposed to the music as well as being taught about the artists.[68]

Although Hale-Benson's strategies are written for use with children, with appropriate age-level modifications this culturally specific model can be used with all ages in any educational setting within the black church.

CONCLUSION

Pastors should develop an understanding of teaching/learning philosophy and understand how their church school teachers approach teaching and learning. It is the teaching/learning philosophy which determines if learning actually takes place.

If a unified approach to Christian education is to exist, it is imperative that some common ground be reached in this area. The church school can grow and prosper if there is unity in the approach to the teaching/learning task.

The teaching/learning strategy for this chapter is a survey to assess whether church school teachers teach from a pedagogical or an andragogical approach. A review of Chapter 1 (page 1) and Appendix A (page 59) will help you determine which responses represent an andragogical or pedagogical response.

Discussion questions are found immediately after the survey. I trust that this material will help to convey the importance of a proper teaching/learning philosophy.

TEACHING/LEARNING STRATEGY SURVEY

This survey may be administered to church school teachers to determine whether their teaching/learning philosophy reflects a pedagogical or an andragogical approach, and it can serve as a discussion starter about teaching/learning philosophy.

(Please check only one response.)

(1) What image comes to mind when you see or hear the term *school?*

❑ Memorizing
❑ A nurturing environment
❑ A loving teacher
❑ Fear of being "called on"
❑ Rewards or punishments
❑ Other: Please specify______________

(2) What does the term *education* mean to you?

❑ The acquisition of knowledge and skills.
❑ Something that enables one to reach full potential as a person in relationship with other persons.
❑ Truth that is poured into someone from the outside.
❑ Other: Please specify______________________________

(3) Which choice best expresses your understanding of your role as a church school teacher and the role of your students?

❑ The students are competitors and the teacher is an authority figure.
❑ The students are colleagues and the teacher is a facilitator of learning.
❑ The students are a resource.
❑ The teacher is a resource.
❑ Other: Please specify______________________________

(4) Which learning setting is most comfortable for you?

❑ A formal setting that is highly competitive.
❑ An informal setting where mutual respect is maintained and needed support is given.
❑ Other: Please specify______________________________

(5) In your classroom, who should plan the learning experience?

❑ The teacher.
❑ The students.
❑ Both teacher and students, through a collaborative process.
❑ Other: Please specify______________________________

(6) In your classroom, who should determine the needs of those involved in the learning experience?

❑ The teacher.
❑ The students.
❑ Both teacher and students, through mutual assessment.
❑ Other: Please specify______________________________

(7) In your classroom, who should set the goals to be achieved through the learning experience?

❑ The teacher.
❑ The students.
❑ Both teacher and students, through mutual negotiation.
❑ Other: Please specify______________________________

(8) In your classroom, who should evaluate the learning experience?
- ❑ The teacher.
- ❑ The students.
- ❑ Both teacher and students, through mutual assessment.
- ❑ Other: Please specify________________________________

(9) What do you feel is the mission of Christian education?
- ❑ To produce knowledgeable Christian persons.
- ❑ To produce competent Christian persons.
- ❑ Other: Please specify________________________________

(10) What do you feel is your mission as a Christian teacher/educator?
- ❑ To operate "successful" educational activities (success being defined in terms of the numbers and enthusiasm of the participants).
- ❑ To help individuals satisfy their needs and achieve their goals.
- ❑ Other: Please specify________________________________

(11) Which statement best sums up your opinion on Christian education?
- ❑ Learning is primarily a function of youth; education supplies individuals in their youth with all the knowledge they will need for the rest of their lives.
- ❑ Learning is a lifelong process.
- ❑ Other: Please specify________________________________

(12) Which definition best expresses your understanding of a "mature Christian person"?
- ❑ A mature Christian person is one who has attained a certain level of achievement and stopped there.
- ❑ A mature Christian person is one who knows a large number of facts about the faith.
- ❑ A mature Christian person is one who has grown in knowledge and in the wise use of it.
- ❑ Other: Please specify________________________________

(13) How do you view the learning process?
- ❑ Learning is active—we are active inquirers after knowledge.
- ❑ Learning is passive—we are passive recipients of knowledge.
- ❑ Other: Please specify________________________________

(14) Which statement best describes your conception of your role as a Christian educator/teacher?
- ❑ I educate and transmit knowledge to others, telling them what they ought to know.
- ❑ I facilitate the learning process and serve as a "change agent," performing a "helping role."
- ❑ Other: Please specify________________________________

(15) Which list of terms best describes your understanding of your role as a Christian educator/teacher?
- ❑ Helper, guide, encourager, consultant, resource.
- ❑ Transmitter, disciplinarian, judge, authority.
- ❑ Other: Please specify________________________________

(16) Indicate whether the following terms represent positive or negative feelings toward education:

(Check only one)

Pos.	Neg.	
❑	❑	(a) School building
❑	❑	(b) Podium on a stage
❑	❑	(c) Chairs placed in a row
❑	❑	(d) Chalkboards
❑	❑	(e) Chairs placed in a circle
❑	❑	(f) Small, informal learning groups

(17) Do you view learning as "proactive" or "reactive"?

❑ Learning is reactive. ❑ I react to information transmitted via books, lectures, etc.

❑ Learning is proactive. ❑ It is a self-directed personal learning style.

❑ Other: Please specify____________________________________

***A special word of thanks to Dr. Anne Wimberly for her help in developing this survey.**

DISCUSSION QUESTIONS

(1) What do you understand *Christian education* to mean?

(2) Do you teach from a pedagogical or andragogical approach? What are the pros and cons of each approach?

(3) What do you understand passive learning and active learning to mean?

(4) Are you utilizing passive learning or active learning in the teaching/learning setting?

(5) What changes have you observed in the behavior of those you teach? Is the change a reflection on your teaching/learning philosophy?

Activity

Write a teaching/learning philosophy. Share your understanding of the role of the teacher and learner in the teaching/learning experience.

Wrap-Up

Closing Prayer

Chapter 5

Teacher Preparation

One reason for membership decline within The United Methodist Church and its church schools may be lack of preparation on the part of church school teachers.

This chapter will examine the problem of inadequate church school teacher preparation as it finds expression within the black church. I will also look at the biblical foundations that demonstrate the need for adequate preparation, as well as the need to engage in ongoing personal study and the need to participate in church school teacher training sessions.

The Effects of Inadequate Teacher Preparation upon the Black Church

Willard A. Williams cites several problem areas that must be addressed to improve the state of Christian education in the black church. First, **biblical illiteracy** is a phenomenon that affects the learned and unlearned; a lack of biblical background affects attendance at Bible classes, etc. Second, **poor teaching methods** contribute to the lack of interest among black people. A third major problem is a **lack of teacher training;** because some church school teachers are incompetent, church school members are lost. Finally, most **curriculum materials do not relate to the lifestyle of black people.**[69]

There are others who share Williams' opinion. Mary A. Love agrees that teacher training and enrichment are essential. To be an effective teacher, one must be an effective student. If we are to train disciples for our Lord Jesus Christ, we must be renewed, refreshed, and enriched. We must have a regular program of teacher training if we expect the black Sunday school to continue its relevance within the black church and community. The Sunday school isn't a separate entity of the local church comprised of only children and youth; it is part of a communal whole that is designed to nurture and to feed all members of the Body of Christ. As Love says, the Sunday school must be seen as a total congregational concern.[70] While the term *church school* indicates a flexibility of time and meeting days, the term *Sunday school* may be more familiar to members of the black church. Love's observations on the Sunday school are applicable to the church school. Because the Sunday school is such an important facet of the black church, the task of teacher preparation and training must not be neglected.

The black church must make a concerted effort to address the problem of inadequate teacher preparation. As noted in Chapter 1, a major problem facing United Methodism is declining membership and a declining church school. Bishop Richard B. Wilke, citing statistics obtained from Warren J. Hartman, says:

> *Most discouraging, in spite of strong efforts in several quarters, is the drop in Sunday School membership by nearly 20,000 and the drop in Sunday School attendance, a more accurate figure, by nearly 60,000. Given the reality that for over a century Sunday School attendance has a three year "lead time" over church membership, we still are in a downward spiral.*[71]

While proper teacher preparation is not a panacea for a declining church school, it is a good starting point for rectifying the problem.

Biblical Foundations That Undergird the Need for Adequate Teacher Preparation

On a cold night in February at United Theological Seminary, our faculty advisor in the Doctor of Ministry Program, Bishop James S. Thomas, commenting on the need for adequate preparation in ministry, said: "God can use ignorance, but sometimes it's even hard for God."[72]

Within the black church school, the temptation is often to rely strictly upon the leading of the Holy Spirit. There are some who fail to do adequate preparation and study because they have fallen prey to this thinking. While I believe in the approach to teaching that affirms "Holy Spirit" inspiration, I believe we are apt to fail if we do not prepare. We must delve into the scriptures to examine the views contained in them regarding proper preparation.

In 2 Timothy 2:15 we hear the words of Paul as spoken to young Timothy. Bennie E. Goodwin II offers an excellent analysis of this text, shedding light on the need for adequate teacher preparation:

> *Probably the most quoted verse among Christian educators is the sentence Paul wrote in his second letter to Timothy. "Study," it says in the King James Version, "to show thyself approved unto God, a workman that needeth not to be ashamed, rightly dividing the word of truth" (2:15). Although the Greek word translated "study" does not really mean study in an academic sense, it does carry with it the general meaning of our word "studious." The Greek word means to "be diligent, be persistently serious about or give concentrated attention to the task."*[73]

Goodwin helps us understand the importance of diligent, serious study. If a church school teacher is to be effective, the task of proper preparation and study must be taken seriously.

Sid Smith cites the example of Jesus to demonstrate the merit of teacher preparation, asserting that Jesus believed in training because *he* was trained and modeled training for others. Jesus trained and educated his followers by precept and by example. Before his followers embarked upon their work, Jesus took them through a training program. Jesus provides us with an excellent example for the training of Sunday school workers.[74]

Smith calls our attention to the Matthew 9 and 10 passage, where six elements of training are found:

1. Training means **helping workers and teachers recognize needs and meet them.** Directing us to Matthew 9:35-10:1, Smith points to Jesus' ministry and to the way he saw everyone with compassion. Jesus saw the harassed, the helpless and the hopeless, and knew they needed a shepherd. After recognizing these profound needs, he called and gave his disciples authority over the unclean and the demonic, and the power to heal diseases and infirmities. This scripture passage demonstrates, dramatically, the meaning and importance of training. Workers and teachers must be able to see persons, recognize their plight, and respond appropriately to their needs, as Jesus did. Training helps workers and teachers see, recognize, and respond.

2. Training means **enabling workers to understand the task in its fullness.** Smith refers to Matthew 10:5-15, where Jesus offers the disciples an orientation before sending them out. Jesus recognized that the disciples needed to fully understand their task and counseled them as follows.

- Know the **audience** (Matt. 10:5-6). Jesus targeted a certain group, "the lost sheep of the house of Israel." Training programs must identify the target group or audience they are attempting to reach.
- Know the kind of **ministry needed** within the context (Matt. 10:7-8). Jesus gave instruction on the types of ministry to be rendered—preaching, teaching, healing the sick, raising the dead, purging lepers, and exorcising demons. Workers and teachers must be holistic in their ministry, showing how the gospel is relevant to the whole of life.
- Keep **priorities** in order and fulfillment will be derived (Matt. 10:9-10). Jesus told his disciples that their primary concern should not be physical sustenance but their *mission.* When a worker or teacher devotes adequate time to lesson preparation, visitation, accurate recordkeeping, planning, attendance at workers' meetings, and prayer, fulfillment will come. The teacher's greatest reward is in seeing persons saved and growing.
- Recipients of ministry also have **responsibilities** (Matt. 10:11-15). While our calling is a tremendous task, the burden is not ours alone. The hearer is obliged to *respond* to the gospel. The teaching/learning experience is a joint venture between teacher and student.

3. Training means **preparing workers for the realities of their task** (Matt. 10:16-23). Jesus prepared the apostles for the hostility and opposition they would face. Ministry is not easy. The challenge before us is to persevere in the face of difficulty.

4. Training means **offering encouragement** to workers and teachers who minister through the Sunday school (Matt. 10:24-33). Jesus encouraged his followers as he sent them out to do their ministry. A good teacher training program focuses on encouraging workers.

5. Training means **presenting accurately the commitment to service that is needed** in order to be effective (Matt. 10:34-39). Jesus never painted a pretty picture of the cost of discipleship. In this passage he describes

the kind of commitment necessary to serve effectively. Jesus knew that anyone who followed him had made a decision that could have severe consequences; thus, the deepest commitment was needed. Those who serve the Sunday school should understand the kind of commitment needed to serve effectively. A half-hearted approach to ministry within the Sunday school will hinder its overall effectiveness.

6. Training means **sharing with fellow workers in the present and eternal rewards of service** (Matt. 10:40-42). Two fundamental truths arise from this passage:

- There is a relationship between receiving Christ's messenger and receiving Christ.
- There are rewards involved in giving service.

Workers and teachers must see the correlation between their ministry and the reception of Christ. They must understand that they are God's instruments and that God works through them. This experience means rewards in this world and in eternity.[75]

Though Smith uses the term *Sunday school,* preparation and training are of paramount importance to the *overall ministry* of the church school.

THE NEED FOR ONGOING PERSONAL STUDY HABITS

If the church school teacher is to be prepared, he or she must have a disciplined life of study. The church school has suffered from the effects of "the Saturday night special," a lesson that is basically thrown together at the last minute. Howard G. Hendricks offers a word of advice to the church school teacher. He advocates maintaining a consistent study/reading program; the teacher must read and then spend an equal amount of time reflecting on that reading, thus helping retention.[76]

The church school teacher faces the same dilemma as the preacher. Week after week, one is called upon to offer something fresh to challenge the community of faith. With such a large responsibility personal growth must be ongoing. The church school teacher must read, study, and reflect in order to stay fresh and creative. The prepared church school teacher will study the scriptures and consult Bible dictionaries, concordances, atlases, commentaries, and lexicons in order to be thorough. Consistent reading/study habits are a must in order to do one's best.

THE IMPORTANCE OF PARTICIPATION IN CHURCH SCHOOL TRAINING SESSIONS

It has been my pleasure to serve in a ministry where church school teachers affirm the validity of church school training sessions.

I believe the congregation must see the commitment of the pastor to the ministry of the church school. As mentioned in Chapter 1, the pastor must participate actively in the life of the church school. Church school teachers are apt to respond favorably when the pastor leads or participates in the teacher training sessions.

Once church school teachers see the pastor's willingness to participate, the enthusiasm will be contagious! Teacher meetings and training sessions can serve as meaningful times of fellowship and sharing that greatly enhance ministry. All churches should work toward creating such sessions on a weekly basis. The sessions will refresh and renew church school teachers as they share their joys, sorrows, burdens, and blessings. I urge all church school teachers to take seriously their responsibility to participate in such regular times of meeting, sharing, and learning.

CONCLUSION

The church school teacher is charged with the responsibility to be prepared. If the quality of the church school within United Methodism is to improve, we must offer every opportunity for persons to enhance their teaching skills. I agree with Dr. E. V. Hill who says that every teacher has three binding obligations: to **be** something, to **know** something, and to **share** something.[77]

A teaching/learning strategy begins on the following page.

TEACHING/LEARNING STRATEGY

Ask each teacher to read 2 Timothy 2:15 and begin a discussion on the following issues:

(1) How is the advice of Paul to Timothy relevant to the task of the church school teacher?

(2) What is each teacher's definition of "study"?

(3) What is each teacher's method of study and how does it apply to teaching?

Learning Activity

Divide the church school teachers into groups and assign the following scripture passages to the groups:

Matthew 9:35-10:1	Matthew 10:5-15	Matthew 10:16-23
Matthew 10:24-33	Matthew 10:34-39	Matthew 10:40-42

Discuss the following issues:

(1) How did Jesus prepare his followers within the context of the scripture?

(2) Do you believe that Jesus valued preparation? Why?

(3) How do the words of Jesus relate to the work of the church school teacher?

Commitment Activity

The facilitator should ask each teacher:

How much time do you spend in preparation for your church school class each week? Would God be pleased?

Wrap-Up

Closing Prayer

Chapter 6

How to Teach a Lesson

The most important task of the church school teacher is to teach the Word of God effectively. There is a sacredness attached to this task; the church school teacher, in most cases, shares more time with parishioners than does the pastor. This means that the teaching task enters the realm of a divine calling. Chapter 6 will examine the effective presentation of the church school lesson, including the use of the Bible, teaching aims, and teaching methods.

Effective Use of the Bible

The beginning point of effective church school teaching is a creative encounter with the Word of God. John H. Westerhoff, III describes the Bible as a **storybook**—a love story between God and humanity. It is a story of a covenant made, broken, and renewed over and over again. God, being the Creator, loves all creatures individually and communally as members of the whole human family. In return, therefore, we are to love God and one another. Westerhoff believes the Bible to be a book of faith that presents a way to perceive life in communal and individual terms. The Bible is also a **book of revelation** that unveils those intimate relationships with God as experienced by others, so that we can share in them. Finally, the Bible is a **book of vocation** that gives us a vision of how we ought to live our lives with God and each other day by day. Westerhoff encourages us to enlarge our grasp of this love story—to learn it more completely, to understand it more deeply, to possess it more personally, and to live it more fully. Westerhoff notes that this is a lifelong task that we begin by learning to tell the story as our story. By doing so, we can transform individual and social life so that God's will may be done and God's kingdom may come.[78]

It is essential that those who teach the Bible embrace its stories as their own story. If the church school hour is to prove meaningful to those who participate in the teaching/learning experience, it must be evident that church school teachers embrace the biblical narrative as their own story. Lawrence O. Richards affirms this by saying that God's Word must be communicated as a lived and livable reality; it must be passed on by those who have integrated it into their personalities and lives.[79]

Sid Smith demonstrates to us the importance of the scriptures as they relate to the growth of Christians. Once the church school teacher has had a living encounter with God, as revealed through the scriptures, he or she must lead other persons toward growth. According to Smith, Bible study contributes to Christian growth in the following ways:

1. **Knowledge of biblical tradition.** The early Christians transmitted the basics of the Christian tradition through teaching. These basics included the sayings of Jesus, his life and ministry, and the Christian interpretations of the Old and New Testaments. Unless we understand the content, structure, literature, thought-forms, and message of the Bible, it is difficult to grow to maturity.

2. **Knowledge of the gospel.** Early Christians concentrated on a proper understanding of the gospel itself; they had a solid understanding of the "plan of salvation." Modern Christians need such an awareness. Our time is characterized by all types of "isms," and the church in the black community is challenged by these things which can be met by an understanding of the gospel. Further, the church can help persons grow out of immaturity through an understanding of the gospel.

3. **Knowledge of the Christian way of life.** The challenges were many for early Christians, as they sought to understand how to apply the gospel. As Christians, they were expected to live under the Lordship of Jesus Christ. As they attempted to integrate faith and practice, they were challenged to define proper standards of Christian conduct. The apostles addressed these problems through teaching. Bible study helps persons understand how Christians should act in different situations. Christianity speaks to such issues as peace, hate, the disenfranchised, personal relationships, racism, stewardship, liberation, and the will of God.[80]

Effective use of the Bible is essential to the church school teacher. As the church school teacher has a continuous living encounter with the Word of God, it will be apparent to those with whom he or she shares on a weekly basis.

TEACHING AIMS

Lowell E. Brown and Bobbie Reed offer advice in the area of teaching aims. Citing the work of Findley B. Edge, Brown and Reed conclude that many church school teachers teach in generalities rather than in specifics. Many feel that the ultimate aim is to teach God's Word in order to see lives conform to the image of Christ. This teaching aim is too general; the church school teacher must define a specific aim for each lesson. Thus, each class session will help the learner through the steps of listening, exploring, discovering, appropriating, and assuming responsibility.[81]

Brown and Reed cite another common error made by church school teachers— setting teaching aims that are lesson-centered rather than person-centered, focusing solely on the transmission of information or "covering the lesson."[82]

Finally, Brown and Reed describe three significant levels of learning: (1) **The Cognitive Level**—the knowledge or information level. The aim of this level is basically to gain factual information. (2) **The Affective Level**—the "feeling level," which includes our emotions and attitudes. The church school teacher must help students "feel" a certain response to a given truth. (3) **The Behavioral Level**—the "response level." The church school teacher can use learning activities to help learners "respond" in a practical way to a new truth.[83]

The challenge for church school teachers is to make the suggested aims—"to know, to feel, to do"—more specific for their classes. They may need to restate printed lesson aims in terms of their own learners. An understanding of specific personal needs leads to effective, specific teaching aims.[84] The clearer the church school teacher is in defining the desired goals, both long- and short-range, the more likely he or she is to employ the correct methodology.[85]

TEACHING METHODS

According to *Foundations,* "Teachers are effective to the degree that they follow the example of Jesus in finding and using teaching methods that will address the unique capacities, experiences, and interests of each student — yet without altering the basic Christian message."[86]

The focus of ongoing educational debate is the question, Which is the better method: passive or active learning? In the black church, I have noticed a great degree of reliance upon the lecture method. Perry G. Downs says that the values of the lecture method are as follows: (1) It is an effective means of communicating content in a systematic manner. Precision and logic are important facets of theological and biblical lectures. (2) It is an efficient use of time, as large amounts of content can be communicated in a relatively short period of time. (3) It affords the teacher the privilege of more direct control. The teacher can control the pace of learning, the terms being used, the direction and emphasis of the study, and the specific points of application.[87]

Downs points out potential problems with the lecture method: (1) A high degree of skill is required to be an effective lecturer. However the potential problem is with the person, not the method. (2) The lecture method does not actively involve the students. However, students must take on responsibility for their own spiritual development. Church school teachers can use a variety of methods, many of which will call for active participation by students; when the lecture method is used, it should promote self-reliance as opposed to dependence on the teacher.[88]

According to Downs, the lecture method is good when the church school teacher is a skilled lecturer and when the class is made up of 15-20 persons. With fewer students, lectures are more difficult to deliver well.[89]

Finally, Downs identifies four keys to making effective use of the lecture method: (1) **Preparation.** Vocal variety, audibility, movement, and enthusiasm all convey proper preparation. (2) **Presentation.** Good posture, eye contact, and vocal control are all a part of presentation. (3) **Concern.** Love for those we teach has to be evident. The goal of teaching is not to impress persons or to demean them for their weaknesses. (4) **Teaching Aids.** The effective use of teaching aids adds variety to the use of the lecture method.[89]

Norma J. Everist echoes many of Downs' observations. She sees the following problems with the lecture method: (1) It is often utilized by those who think it to be the *only* teaching style. When overused, it promotes passivity rather than active involvement in the learning process. (2) It is often used in predictable ways. Predictable learning produces comfort, which ultimately results in passivity. (3) Lecturers sometimes fail to turn themselves off again once they are turned on. The thrill of hearing one's own voice engages the mind; meanwhile, our listeners find theirs dulled. (4) Lectures provide only one point of view. Although a variety of resources have been consulted, the lecture method normally means the construction of a clear statement of issues. Real learning, however, takes place when students gain exposure to a wide variety of ideas. (5) A lecture only engages the ears of the learner—the learner must construct questions about the lecture, thus negating the students' capacity for creative thought and contribution.[90]

Everist offers these basic guidelines for the lecture: (1) The purpose of the lecture method is to inform. The effective lecturer can bring information together in new and relevant ways that the printed page cannot. (2) The lecturer should assume that learners want to hear. A church school teacher who exhibits enthusiasm in teaching will encourage growth in his or her students. (3) A lecturer must utilize the best possible grammar, diction, and vocabulary. If we are going to use the lecture method, we should do it well. (4) The lecture is for people. Those to whom we lecture should be our ultimate concern.[91]

Finally, Everist points out that lectures can be properly used at every age level, although the lecture method is often reserved for those who teach adult classes. Everist examines the use of lecture with various age groups:

(1) Brief, concrete mini-lectures can be used with **young children.** Story is not the only means for young children to receive biblical material.

(2) Ten-minute presentations of new material to **elementary age children** can be effective, especially among upper elementary children (9-12 years old) who are fascinated with new ideas, facts, and broader horizons.

(3) Lecture is effective with **teens** because they are dealing with abstract concepts and wrestling with deep faith issues. When used with other methods, the lecture method can provide wide enough boundaries for broad-ranging ideas, while still being within the community of faith.

(4) Lecture should be used thoughtfully and sparingly with **adults** because adults have grown conditioned to passivity in learning.[92]

While lecture can be an acceptable method, I am inclined to agree with Howard G. Hendricks: "Maximum learning is always the result of maximum involvement."[93] We must find ways to actively involve students in the learning process. John C. Elias says it has always been a goal of education to develop learning models that closely approximate real-life situations, from which people learn the most. An active approach might include:

Role Playing — The spontaneous portrayal or acting out of a particular situation by a group. This normally results in a discussion to determine the relationships between the characters.

Case Method — This method analyzes a problem, applying what is learned to a particular situation in life.

Demonstration — This teaching method involves showing and telling how something is done. It encourages participation, as well as helping to instill confidence and interest in the performance of a specific function.[94]

CONCLUSION

The church school teacher has a tremendous resource available—a creative mind. The church school lesson must be prepared in such a way that it encourages student involvement through activity, reflection, and interaction. Students will look forward to the church school hour with excitement when they know that activity, not passivity, is the watchword.

A teaching/learning strategy is included on the following page. Appendix C, page 71, includes a teaching plan developed by Dr. Richard E. Allison of Ashland Theological Seminary. This plan will help your church school teachers pull together the concepts presented in this chapter.

TEACHING/LEARNING STRATEGY

Note: This learning activity can be modified for use with children and youth.

Ask each church school teacher to describe his or her method of teaching a church school lesson. After giving each teacher an opportunity to respond, ask each to reflect on these questions:

(1) What are the advantages and disadvantages to utilizing the lecture method?

(2) Does your approach allow for active participation?

Ask each teacher to discuss his/her opinions on these issues with the entire group.

LEARNING ACTIVITY

Each church school teacher should select a teacher training session in which he or she will teach the week's church school lesson according to the teaching plan in Appendix C, page 71. While this activity will take several weeks to complete, it is helpful in the following ways:

(1) It helps the facilitator assess the teaching methods of the particular church school teacher (the facilitator may opt to use an evaluation).

(2) It helps to expand the creativity of the other church school teachers as they observe the methods of their colleagues.

(3) It helps to formulate a team concept in the church school.

After each teacher has taught during one of the weekly sessions, time should be allotted for general reflections on this teaching/learning experience. I offer two possible questions to be raised:

How did you grow as a result of the teaching/learning experience?

How might this teaching/learning experience strengthen your classroom performance?

Wrap-Up

Closing Prayer

CHAPTER 7

EVANGELISM AS IT RELATES TO THE CHURCH SCHOOL

Church school is an excellent starting point for cultivating evangelistic efficacy and, perhaps thereby, for addressing the issue of membership decline.

The black church within United Methodism has a rich evangelistic heritage, with its roots firmly grounded in the Wesleyan tradition. The following chapter examines the distinctive nature of evangelism among black people and the relationship of evangelism to the teaching task and to the ministry of the church school.

THE HISTORIC ROLE OF EVANGELISTIC MOVEMENTS AMONG BLACK PEOPLE

The Sunday school has always been linked to the task of evangelism, whether evangelism meant "indoctrination" or represented a genuine attempt to proclaim God's grace as it found expression in the life, death, and resurrection of Jesus Christ. To many scholars of the history of the black church in America, the Sunday school was used to "Christianize" enslaved Africans, to bring about their acceptance of slave status. Paul Nichols notes the involvement of The Society for the Propagation of the Gospel in this process:

> *The Society for the Propagation of the Gospel (SPG) figured prominently in the call for religious instruction among blacks. In keeping with their objective to convert the so-called heathen to the Christian faith, the SPG naturally turned its attention to the black slaves in America, who were numbered among the heathen.*[95]

In the late 1700s and throughout the 1800s, a change occurred in the purpose of the black Sunday school. It became the setting where slaves learned to read and write, allowing them to see the gospel in a new light. The gospel became relevant to the black experience; this reinterpretation of the gospel started a new trend, and the organization of many local congregations soon followed.[96]

If we take our examination to a deeper level, it should be noted that the Wesleyan movement sought to do more than merely indoctrinate; it presented a sincere and simple call to righteousness. Black Americans responded favorably to Methodism because of its evangelistic appeal and because of the Methodist attitude toward slavery.[97] Frederick A. Norwood notes that John Wesley, the Father of Methodism, out of commitment to his doctrinal beliefs, objected to the evil of slave trade. Wesley and William Wilberforce actively worked for the abolition of slave trade in the British Empire. Thomas Coke was of the same mind as Wesley on this matter.[98]

Historians note that Coke was virtually mobbed in Virginia as a result of his strong anti-slavery stands. Coke persisted in speaking against slavery, which led to his life being threatened and lawsuits being filed against him. Coke joined Asbury in addressing a petition to George Washington on behalf of Methodists for emancipation of slaves in Virginia. Coke recorded with pleasure in his journal the fact that Washington was sympathetic with the Methodist position.[99]

William B. McClain asserts that black Americans recognized the Wesleyan evangelical message as a sincere call to righteousness. The evangelical message of the Methodist movement sought "to awaken a godly experience in its hearers of a conscious fellowship with God."[100] The message's emphasis was upon the love of God and the way of redemption. Poor benighted sinners were told of a Father who cares for all of his children. This message of salvation, love, redemption, and hope helped a pilgrim people embrace a sustaining faith. The evangelistic experience was vital to black Americans who were searching for meaning, purpose, and hope in life.

The Distinctive Nature of Evangelism Among Black People

The vast differences among cultural and ethnic groups must be acknowledged if evangelism is to be effective. Evangelism in the church school must design a ministry that considers the distinctive nature of the black experience in America. Glenn C. Smith stresses the need for churches to acknowledge the distinct evangelistic needs of black Americans:

> *To reach black Americans for Jesus Christ requires the would-be evangelizer to realize that vast differences exist and thereby the methods must differ as well. Legitimate cultural differences exist between blacks and whites, between Hispanics and orientals. What works for one group simply will not work with the others. Black America has a deep spiritual heritage that differs dramatically with that of most white parishes. The denomination that would seek to evangelize unchurched black Americans will need to know and accept their history, their culture, their manner of worship, and their distinct religious expression.*[101]

Wallace Charles Smith states that, historically, the black family has been an inclusive community, as well as an adoptionist community. It is within this context that evangelism was done in the black church. When a sinner was saved, this meant inclusion into membership and the grafting into that church of a new family member who became a full participant in the life and customs of the church.[102]

THE RELATIONSHIP OF EVANGELISM TO THE TEACHING TASK

Every church school teacher should be able to put into historical perspective the impact of evangelism on the black religious experience. Once the enslaved black men and women experienced "pure" evangelism, filled with its message of freedom and liberation, they embraced the Christian faith and sought to live out its teachings and principles.

The church school has the obligation to fulfill the Great Commission as given by Jesus to his disciples:

> *Go therefore and make disciples of all nations, baptizing them in the name of the Father and of the Son and of the Holy Spirit, and teaching them to obey everything that I have commanded you. And, remember, I am with you always, to the end of the age.* (Matthew 28:19-20)

The church school teacher is granted a tremendous evangelistic opportunity each week. Roy H. Ryan states that selecting an appropriate teaching/learning strategy should be a major concern of the church. Ryan asserts that the style of witnessing and methodology used to teach should be compatible with the teacher's understanding of the gospel, the age of those being taught, and an approach that is theologically, biblically, and psychologically sound. According to Ryan, the teaching task involves telling one's own story. Every Christian has a unique faith journey, an individual pilgrimage of faith. The church school teacher can certainly utilize curriculum resources to guide the teaching process, but the lesson becomes lively and personal when our own story is included. Teaching at its best occurs when the lesson is embodied or "the Word becomes flesh."[103]

James O. Stallings concurs with Ryan, articulating the need for black Americans to tell their individual faith stories. An evangelism group in his church examined the presence and movement of God in their lives and explored how to communicate those encounters effectively. Stallings reports that several members deemed their faith story to be insignificant. The tendency of some within the group was to use "religious talk"— those popular, nice, pious clichés that are often heard among church members. These clichés, Stallings states, are often confusing to church members, although it is assumed that everyone will understand them. Once the group was able to sift through the religious talk, members were able to focus on significant experiences of God's work in their lives.

Stallings further reports that this teaching/learning experience validated the authority of personal experiences. These persons spoke with integrity as they shared with others their experiences of the work of the Spirit in their lives. They listened to others and were heard themselves. This helped the members of the group discern the activity of God within the lives of other persons, calling forth a change of attitude and discipline.[104]

It is important for the church school teacher to tell his or her story to the church school class and to connect that story with the biblical story, an invitation toward faith and discipleship. The teaching/learning experience is an excellent opportunity for persons to accept Jesus Christ as their Savior and Lord.

Sid Smith believes that the growth-oriented Sunday school is an evangelistic movement that seeks to win the lost to Christ. The teaching task is intimately related to the work of evangelism and Bible teaching yields evangelistic results for the following reasons:

(1) **Bible study brings about living encounters with the Word of God.** Smith refers to the story of the Ethiopian eunuch in Acts 8 in which a black man was prepared to receive Christ through a living encounter with the scriptures. Many persons are won to Christ as they consider the Word of God and appropriate it to their lives.

(2) **Bible study provides an interpersonal climate** which is conducive to decisions for Christ. Bible study provides a climate for *koinonia,* New Testament fellowship. Persons who participate in Bible study share more than information; they share and enter into the hurts, joys, and life experiences of their fellow pilgrims.

(3) **Bible study generates a genuine concern for the lost.** Studying the scriptures strengthens the desire to help the unsaved. If the vast number of persons who need to be saved are to be saved, they must hear the gospel. The Bible helps Christians understand their call to evangelize the lost.

(4) **Bible study programs provide a logical structure for evangelistic outreach.** The growth-oriented Sunday school seeks to evangelize all prospects from the community. Because the Sunday school should be organized to include every age group, it represents a logical structure for the sharing of the gospel.

(5) **Bible study groups provide a context for assimilating new converts into the church fellowship.** When persons have a conversion experience, they need nurture and growth as they seek their place of service within the church. The Sunday school is a place where significant relationships can be formulated by new members as they are assimilated into the fellowship circle of the church.[105]

Vincie Alessi states:

> *It is the task of evangelism to (1) bring all persons into living, active fellowship with God through Jesus Christ as divine Savior and Lord; (2) gather all persons, through the regenerating power of the Holy Spirit, into the fellowship of the church; (3) lead persons to express their Christian discipleship in every area of human life so that the kingdom of God may be realized.*[106]

Finally, we cannot conclude our consideration without emphasizing the need for the Holy Spirit's presence in the life and ministry of the church school teacher. As the church school teacher seeks the appropriate evangelistic strategy and prepares for the teaching task, he or she must be sensitive to the leading of the Holy Spirit. William B. McClain says it well:

> *It is because we have been seized by the Holy Spirit and experienced the divine commission that we must witness to the saving power of the gospel, the reality of the divine liberation, that we must "tell the story" of our experience. It is good news because we have been brought out of darkness into light, from bondage to freedom and we must share it with others.*[107]

Church school teachers must be Spirit-led as they prepare the teaching/learning experience.

CONCLUSION

Evangelism has always been a focal point of the black religious experience and represents a priority of the church school. The church school teacher must approach the evangelistic task with methods that are appropriate for African American persons. If this is done correctly, the church school will grow and enrollment will increase. But most important of all, souls will be won to Jesus Christ.

TEACHING/LEARNING STRATEGY

In *Reaching the Black Community Through the Sunday School,* Sid Smith states: "Bible teaching is foundational in building people in Christ. The Word of God provides the diet through which growing Christians thrive. Churches do not maximally grow apart from the knowledge of the Word. True evangelism does not happen without the redemptive message from the Bible. Edification of Christians is rooted and grounded in the presence of the Word in their lives."[108]

Teaching is at the core of evangelism. (As a group, explore the following scriptures.)

1. Consider the example of Jesus, a unique teacher whose teaching contained an evangelistic thrust. Jesus taught to bring persons to repentance and faith. Look at Matt. 19:16-22.

   > *Jesus proved, questioned, and challenged this young man's presuppositions, attitudes, and values. The bottom line in the lesson was for the ruler to come and follow Jesus. Although the pupil "went away sorrowful," the purpose of the teaching opportunity to Jesus was clearly evangelistic.*[109]

2. Consider the example of the early disciples in Acts 4:2. This teaching was intended for evangelistic results. Discuss the relationship between teaching and evangelism.

3. Read Acts 8:26-39.

The example of Phillip and the Ethiopian eunuch focuses on the relationship between teaching and evangelism. The Ethiopian was reading the works of an Old Testament prophet but with limited understanding. He needed a teacher. Phillip taught him and "told him the good news of Jesus" (Acts 8:35). The result of the lesson was the conversion of this black brother.[110]

We should also note that the early evangelists saw the relationship between teaching and evangelism and utilized it in their strategy for spreading the gospel.

4. Read Acts 14:1; 17:4, 18:4, 26.

These passages show that the early evangelists went into the synagogues (the places of religious instruction and teaching) to proclaim the gospel of Christ.

> *Paul used teaching as a part of his missionary strategy. In Acts 18:11, Paul was on a missionary journey at Corinth and spent "a year and six months, teaching the Word of God among them." Paul evangelized through teaching.*[111]

The main point is that evangelistic teaching is obviously the New Testament approach. The church school should practice teaching that seeks to lead people to God through Christ Jesus.[112]

LEARNING ACTIVITY

As a way of helping church school teachers tell "their story," ask them to share with the group how God has been present in their lives. As a facilitator, help each church school teacher relate his or her story to the teaching task and share the story in evangelistic fashion.

Discussion

Ask the church school teachers the following questions:

(1) As we seek to evangelize, where are identifiable prospects we can contact for church school enrollment?

(2) Can you compile a prospect list?

(3) Are you willing to participate in evangelistic visitation for the church school?

Wrap-Up

Prayer

CHAPTER 8

THE ROLE OF THE CHURCH SCHOOL TEACHER AS A CAREGIVER

The church of Jesus Christ has been subjected to much criticism in recent years due to the "fall" of some noted television evangelists. Yet the work and mission of the church have continued. The church has sought to give care to the bruised and broken in the spirit of Jesus Christ.

In the black community specifically, the church has offered care that has affected the moral climate of the society. Those who are actively involved in the church are less likely to participate in criminal activity. As a study by the National Baptist Business League shows, black youths who attend church on a regular basis are not as likely to become involved in crime. Of the 500 young people between the ages of eight and eighteen surveyed who didn't attend church, 50 percent had been arrested at least once. Of those surveyed who did attend church, only 10 percent had experienced an encounter with the law.[113]

When the black church touches lives in a caring way, a change can be seen throughout our communities and the society as a whole. The church is a caregiving body that can make needed changes in the moral and spiritual climate of our nation. The church school must focus its attention on giving care to the black family. Dr. J. Alfred Smith, Sr. offers this advice:

> *A touchstone for the black church, in addressing the many problems facing the black family and community, is whether the church is prepared to implement programs to deal with the whole needs of a person, of a family, both physical and spiritual. If we are to beseech the black family to return to the church, then the church has to know how to meet black family needs. Our churches, all churches, must have sense and soul.*[114]

As we consider caregiving within the black church, the natural starting place is the church school. If the church is going to meet the full range of needs of people, it begins by knowing them as individuals. With the time limitations of the Sunday morning worship hour, the church school tends to be the better forum for entering into meaningful relationships with persons. Therefore, the needs of the black family can best be ascertained within the church school, under the leadership of a caregiving teacher.

THE BLACK SUNDAY SCHOOL AND ITS HISTORICAL IMPACT THROUGH CAREGIVING

A term that best identifies the black Sunday school with the historical plight of African Americans is *survival.* The black Sunday school has made the gospel relevant to the struggles of an oppressed people. When African Americans have needed acceptance, love, self-worth, self-esteem, and care, they have found these in the black church and in the black Sunday school. These organizations have helped black people to survive in an environment that has sought to dehumanize them. William R. Johnson lends insight into the importance of survival for the African American:

> *Survival was of paramount importance because if one is freed, and one is not able to maintain his/her presence in a society, freedom then is of little consequence and without substance. So it was that the black church saw a part of its mandate for being, that of providing a methodology for survival, and this methodology of survival included that of the founding of predominantly black denominations and black churches through which black people would be able to come together and to find solutions to their immediate problems.*[115]

The black church and black Sunday school have always represented a haven of hope for those seeking to survive. As we approach the year 2000, the black church must look for new, creative ways to offer support and care to African Americans in their struggle to survive.

THE CHURCH SCHOOL TEACHER AS A CAREGIVER

The needs of the black family today can best be assessed within the church school, under the skilled and able leadership of a caregiving teacher. To do so, the church school teacher must cultivate the appropriate atmosphere. The church school class must be a nonthreatening environment in which persons feel welcomed by the other class members. This involves a willingness to listen and share in a nonjudgmental manner. Persons will share their hurts and pains if they know they will not be judged but encouraged to continue their pilgrimage.

The church school teacher is charged with the responsibility of helping students to be good listeners and to detect the hurts of a fellow believer. This requires the development of sensitivity; the church school teacher must pray for the Holy Spirit's guidance in detecting those who need care.

John H. Westerhoff, III, discusses the differences between an institutional church and a community of faith. He stresses the need for depth of relationships and caring; the church school that seeks to give care should consider his thought:

> *In an institutional church human needs are met by someone assigned that responsibility; but in a community of faith, activities can be put aside so that the whole community can respond to individual needs and thereby demonstrate the depth of relationship that is integral to community life.*[116]

Westerhoff also talks about the lack of emotional demands that is characteristic of institutional life. Relationships within the institutions, Westerhoff says, are goal- and task-oriented; acts of caring for the needs of others are limited and extracurricular. Westerhoff concludes that, if the church operates with depth of relationships as families do, then this necessitates and encourages honest and open sharing of emotions and concern for each individual's condition.[117]

Building on Westerhoff's insight, it is the task of the church school teacher to facilitate the formation of relationships. There is a great temptation on the part of many church school teachers to become so task-oriented that they neglect the forming of relationships which marks the beginning of the caregiving process. There are two reasons for this: (1) If no significant relationship exists between the church school teacher and student, then it is unlikely the student will share openly with the church school teacher. (2) If no significant relationships exist among the students in the class, it is unlikely that trust and other necessary caregiving traits will be present.

It is important, then, for the church school teacher to know when to lay aside the task and to give care. Putting away a prepared lesson in order to talk with class members about their needs can be quite rewarding, for these are truly times when all persons share from their "heart of hearts."

One of the most impressive writers in the area of caregiving is Duane A. Ewers. In a chapter on the role of the church school teacher as a caregiver Ewers cites six caregiving gifts that are important to the ministry of the church school teacher— availability, listening, faith-sharing, carefronting, empathy, and preparation for teaching.[118]

1. **Availability** means that the church school teacher is nonjudgmental and offers caring support. The church school teacher demonstrates a willingness to listen and take time to hear the concerns of people. Ewers says that the church school teacher can best be available by resisting the temptation of becoming consumed by "what has to be done next." In addition, availability means being willing to visit a student's home or stay after a class session as needed.[119]

Carlyle Fielding Stewart III, who offers a useful model for prophetic ministry in the African American tradition, says: "Comforting often means demonstrating availability and a willingness to listen to the struggles and trials of a life experience. Verbalizing is often not required, but presence and tenderness go a long way in helping people recover from their hurts, pain, and guilt."[120]

2. "Care-full" **listening** fosters warmth and trust, while calming negative feelings. It helps persons sort out confused, jumbled thoughts. Finally, listening frees up persons and provides space so they can hear the still, small voice of Christ within. Listening opens the door so persons both hear and value the faith story they have to share.[121]

Donald B. Rogers says three things about listening: (1) Listening to learners is an extremely valuable way to establish relevance in education programming. (2) Attentive listening is a valuable teaching process. (3) Training listeners should be one of the first leadership development objectives for the church.[122]

3. Through **faith-sharing,** the church school teacher can invite persons to claim their baptism and to accept Jesus Christ as their Savior and Lord; he/she can challenge students to be faithful disciples by being responsible Christians in their community. Finally, Ewers says that students should be urged to engage in personal Bible study and prayer, to be more caring in

church and community, and to be open to the Holy Spirit's guidance and sustaining presence.[123]

Faith-sharing is a caregiving gift that is relevant to all age levels. MaryJane Pierce Norton stresses the importance of sharing our faith with children:

> *It may be a trite saying, but it's true: we are always one generation away from the extinction of the Christian faith. By teaching invitationally, we invite children to see in words and example the faith of biblical persons, of persons in our church and community, and of our class. We invite children to express freely their own faith by talking together, by teaching them actions that reflect that faith, and by inviting their friends to be with them in Sunday school and worship. We help the next generation live out their faith and teach it to others through words and examples.*[124]

By sharing the faith, we ensure that children will live out their faith and positively influence the world for Christ. This principle applies to all ages; the faith must be shared with *all* persons.

4. **Carefronting** means caring for persons of any age who exhibit self-destructive behavior. Ewers gives these suggestions to the church school teacher who is carefronting:

(a) Offer specific, clear expectations ahead of time to minimize the potential for conflict.
(b) Confront *in private.*
(c) Describe the behavior. Let the person know his or her behavior is causing a problem; state this clearly.
(d) Keep the unacceptable behavior before the person. Whatever the cause, the unacceptable behavior cannot continue. The person should be asked what he/she intends to do about the behavior.[125]

5. **Empathy** is the ability to enter into the sufferings of another, to *feel with* and to understand. Edward P. Wimberly speaks of the pastoral counselor/therapist showing empathy; his thought relates to the church school teacher, who also performs a therapeutic function:

> *The therapist can communicate this empathy by being fully human himself or herself and not giving purely mechanical responses and only intellectual understanding. Empathy is not a technique or an academic skill, but is an experiential quality developed as one learns to be one's genuine self.*[126]

6. **Teaching preparation** means thorough and complete preparation that maximizes the classroom experience and makes the time between teacher and student meaningful. The caring church school teacher studies long and hard to be the best he or she can be.[127]

CONCLUSION

Caregiving is an important component of the church school teacher's ministry and must be taken seriously.

TEACHING/LEARNING STRATEGY

In an often uncaring world, we all need to experience love, nurture, and care.

The church school affords us a unique opportunity to meet the needs of persons facing life's complexities. Those we serve in the church school bring to our context their hurts, hopes, and fears; they also bring their joys, triumphs, and testimonies of God's goodness. This is why the teacher in the church school should be sensitive to both expressed and unexpressed signals that persons send out when they need care.

The church school provides parishioners with a more intimate forum than does the worship service. It is within this setting that church school teachers have one of their greatest opportunities, the opportunity to care. And for teachers to be effective caregivers, they must be intentional about planning and acting in caring ways; this must be a part of their teaching plan and strategy. Ewers says: "I believe that when God calls persons to teach, he also calls them to care."[128]

The scriptures report the very caring nature of God. Read the following passages aloud (this can be done by all persons): Psalm 55:22 and 1 Peter 5:7. These passages demonstrate the magnificent ways in which God renders love and care to us all. If we believe that God uses other persons to express and embody divine love and care for us, then we will be able to see why the gift of caregiving is so vital and needed.

Caregiving as a Gift

Ask a church school teacher to volunteer to read aloud 1 Peter 4:10, a passage which sheds light upon our calling to share our caring gifts with others.

Learning Activity

Ask each teacher to do the following:

(1) Share a recent opportunity that you had to be a caregiver to someone in need. What were the circumstances? How was your caregiving received? What was the result?

(2) Share with the group what you feel are your caring gifts (skills or abilities). What makes it easier or more difficult for you to be a caregiver?

Wrap-Up

Closing Prayer

CHAPTER 9

TEACHING/LEARNING ENVIRONMENT

One of the most neglected areas in Christian education in the black church is the environment in which teaching and learning takes place. This results because: (1) Christian education has not been a high priority for many black churches, so the needs in this area are either ignored or neglected; (2) Christian education in the black church has concerned itself more with the content of teaching than with examining ways to make teaching and learning more effective.

But the teaching/learning environment causes us to be an inclusive or non-inclusive church. As we consider older adults and persons with disabilities, we must be sure the teaching/learning environment bids them welcome. This is why the church school staff and teachers are obligated to look closely and critically at the teaching/learning environment.

WHY IS THE TEACHING/LEARNING ENVIRONMENT SO IMPORTANT?

Lois M. Runk tells us that, before learning can take place, persons must know that they are loved, appreciated, and respected. Every person must know he or she is a child of God and worthy of the love of others. It is important to children that we know their names and greet them as they enter the classroom. We need to spend one-on-one time with children in order to know what is happening in their lives. Runk contends that, when children are accepted, they will participate fully in whatever activities are a part of the teaching/learning experience.[129]

Though Runk addresses her comments to the needs of children, these truths apply to persons of all ages. We all need to know we are unique, and that the church school teacher cares about us and is willing to get to know us. When we feel accepted and valued, we are more apt to participate in the life of the church school.

Runk also deals with the broad scope of the teaching/learning environment. We tend to think only in terms of the *physical* environment (chairs, floors, tables, climate, etc.) when, in fact, the teaching/learning environment includes much more. If this environment is spiritually cold, and persons do not feel welcome, comfortable seats and carpet on the floors will not make much difference. People from all walks of life must feel welcome. If the atmosphere makes persons feel loved, appreciated, and respected, they will be ready to take part in the teaching/learning experience.

THE CLASSROOM ENVIRONMENT CONVEYS CARE

When a teaching/learning environment begins with the love, acceptance, and respect of persons, we can then extend this warmth through the physical environment in the church school. MaryJane Pierce Norton offers good advice on this subject:

> *The space where teaching and learning takes place is important. The way a room looks reflects our feelings about the importance of the people who gather in that space and the importance of what happens in that space. Take time to go to your church and walk through all the rooms. Which ones show the most care? Which ones always look clean? Which ones are free of clutter, have up-to-date bulletin boards, and no old, broken equipment?*[130]

The appearance of the physical environment indicates to people whether we care or not. It is the task of the church school to continue the caregiving process by working hard to make the physical environment as comfortable as possible.

Every congregation must examine the church school to see if it is being used in the most effective way. Kennon L. Callahan talks about the need for determining what is adequate space, especially for the children in the church school:

> *Two factors affect the adequacy of the nursery and kindergarten area: (a) space and (b) design. With regard to space, most churches mistakenly think that since children are smaller than adults they need less space; they then pick the smallest room that can be found for the nursery, place some cribs very close together, and assume that this will be adequate. This assumption is erroneous.*
>
> *Children frequently need more space than adults, whether they be in the nursery, toddler, or kindergarten age range or somewhat older. The key point about space is to analyze the extent to which these spaces provide for the range of activities for nursery, toddler, and kindergarten children.*[131]

Callahan helps us understand that we must make maximum use of spaces that are best suited for the needs of a particular age group.

Wright Pillow and Jennie Youngblood address the common dilemma of somewhat limited resources in the black church. They urge us to make wise, creative use of available space, rather than becoming frustrated over what we do not have. It is exciting to see a well-used, well-kept, attractive church building. Effective use of space and evidence of ongoing study in classrooms and class space cause the advocates of quality teaching to rejoice. The challenge, therefore, is to evaluate the teaching/learning environment, make needed improvements, and use the space wisely.[132]

STRATEGIES TO HELP IMPROVE THE TEACHING/LEARNING ENVIRONMENT

When, in my ministry, we needed to assess the needs of the congregation regarding the teaching/learning environment, we developed the survey in Appendix A, page 59. Using this survey helped us foster total congregational involvement in the church school. The key to bringing about improvement in the teaching/learning environment lies in involving a variety of persons in the strategy sessions.

We interviewed persons with disabilities to see what practical steps we could take to improve the teaching/learning environment. When we had improved seating arrangements and handicap access, teachers and students benefited from a heightened awareness of the need to be inclusive of all persons.

Roy H. Ryan says we need to walk through the facilities to observe the physical conditions of the rooms and equipment. Notes should be taken on equipment/supplies that need to be repaired or replaced and rooms that need redecorating. Special attention should be given to making sure that furnishings and equipment are age-appropriate, comfortable, attractive, and in good condition. Is the space adequate for the class using it? Could vacant space be used? Are the facilities accessible to all persons and up to community codes? Is the church library adequate to the needs of the congregation? Ryan also talks about the need to involve trustees in the whole process, making them aware of all needs; the Finance Committee should be made aware of budgetary needs in this area.[133]

In the black church, as in all churches, financial constraints are an issue. It is crucial that pastoral leadership clearly identify the church school as a ministerial and fiscal priority. This means the pastor should work directly with the Finance Committee. The congregation has to see a commitment on the part of the pastoral leadership if it is to embrace a vision for Christian education.

CONCLUSION

I have attempted to lift up the importance of the teaching/learning environment. As Myrtle Felkner says:

> *An attractive and cheerful environment is a powerful aid for learning. When babies are laid on soiled sheets in a nursery and children with bare legs play on a cold and drafty floor, you may be sure that environment is also speaking loud and clear. Our caring for the comfort and well-being of others is a form of Christian witness.*[134]

The improvement of the teaching/learning environment represents another opportunity to care for the people of God.

TEACHING/LEARNING STRATEGY

The facilitator should help church school teachers think critically about their teaching/learning environment. Ask each teacher to consider these questions as discussion starters:

(1) How do you attempt to make the teaching/learning environment conducive to the needs of special people (such as persons with physical disabilities)?

(2) How does the teaching/learning environment convey to church school students that you care?

Learning Activity

Take a tour of each church school classroom and make these assessments:

(1) Is the furniture appropriate for the age level you teach?

(2) Is there adequate space for each age level?

(3) Is the furniture comfortable?

(4) Is the room temperature comfortable?

(5) What repairs are needed on equipment?

(6) What visual aids are needed to enhance the teaching/learning environment?

(7) Is this room appealing to visitors to the church school?

Wrap-Up

Closing Prayer

CONCLUDING STATEMENT

It is my hope that *Christian Education for the African American Community* represents a significant beginning point for those in black congregations who want to begin or strengthen church school teacher programs. This work is an humble attempt to offer a model based on a particular ministry which may have broader application in other church schools in black churches. While all church schools in the black church are not identical, there is a commonality in the experience of the church school in the black tradition. I have attempted to offer a way to address issues central to the effectiveness of the church school.

I do not view this text as necessarily universal in its appeal or in its application; it is essential that any body of material be modified according to context. This means that any pastor, church school superintendent, Christian education director, seminary student, or conference staff person who reads this work should use it with discretion. I suggest that significant time be devoted to observing what happens in your context and engaging in creative dialogue about your particular educational needs. This is crucial because people are anxious to know their experience is valid and their voice heard. It is also crucial because people are more eager to be engaged in ministry when they can claim ownership.

It is important for black congregations to make the ministry of Christian education a spiritual and fiscal priority. The worship experience, which is the focal point of the black religious tradition, is a marvelous forum for advocating the cause of Christian education. We must also direct our stewardship more toward education. This means that when we set our church budgets we cannot give the appearance that church school and Christian education are mere afterthoughts. In addition, as we think about building great edifices for worship, we may consider building lesser edifices and devoting some of our resources to constructing Christian education facilities.

Above all, remember that this entire process should be undergirded by prayer, sustained through patience, and maintained by hard work and perseverance. In doing these things, we are being faithful to the task to which we are called by Jesus Christ.

APPENDIX A

Note: This survey is to be completed by all persons within your congregation. In an effort to foster participation, persons may be encouraged to complete the survey in a situation where there is an opportunity for food and fellowship.

The following survey contains questions to assess the attitudes and needs of this congregation in the areas of Christian education and church school ministries. Please respond to each question so that an accurate measure of your attitudes and needs can be made. Please do not sign your name. Thank you very much for your participation!

(Check only one response.)

(1) Have you found your past experiences in the church school learning setting to be:
- ❑ Positive
- ❑ Negative
- ❑ Other: Please specify________________________________

(2) As you reflect on past experiences in the church school setting, what do you remember and appreciate about those who taught you?
- ❑ They exhibited mutuality as they taught.
- ❑ They demonstrated love and concern for me.
- ❑ They provided me with information about the Christian faith.

(3) When you see or hear the term *school,* what image comes to mind?
- ❑ Memorization
- ❑ Fear of being "called on"
- ❑ A nurturing environment
- ❑ Rewards or punishments
- ❑ A loving teacher
- ❑ Other: Please specify________________________________

(4) What does the term *education* mean?
- ❑ Education is the acquisition of knowledge and skills.
- ❑ Education is a process of addressing problems and challenges through shared inquiry.
- ❑ Education is truth that is poured into someone from the outside.
- ❑ Other: Please specify________________________________

(5) What is your present opinion of this congregation's church school program and its effectiveness?
- ❑ Good
- ❑ Fair
- ❑ Needs improvement
- ❑ Other: Please specify________________________________

(6) As a person involved in learning, do you learn best by:
- ❑ Being solely dependent upon the teacher for learning?
- ❑ Seeking information and resources and learning independently?
- ❑ Dependence upon teachers, as well as your own ability to gather information and resources to learn independently?
- ❑ Other: Please specify________________________________

(7) As a person involved in learning, do you see your experience as:
- ❑ Irrelevant to the learning experience.
- ❑ Relevant to the learning experience.
- ❑ A rich resource for learning.
- ❑ Other: Please specify______________________________

(8) As a person involved in learning, what makes you eager (or ready) to learn?
- ❑ Your acquired level of maturity.
- ❑ A specific problem that you must resolve.
- ❑ A specific task that you must do.
- ❑ Other: Please specify______________________________

(9) As a person involved in learning, in which setting are you the most comfortable?
- ❑ A setting where specific subjects are studied in logical development.
- ❑ A setting where an individual's particular problems are considered.
- ❑ A setting where particular tasks an individual needs to accomplish are considered.
- ❑ Other: Please specify______________________________

(10) What motivates you to learn?
- ❑ External rewards (money, success, etc.).
- ❑ Punishments.
- ❑ Curiosity (the desire within to know more).
- ❑ Other: Please specify______________________________

(11) When you experience learning, do you apply what you've learned to life?
- ❑ At a later time ("I'll learn algebra now so that I can do calculus later.").
- ❑ Immediately.
- ❑ Other: Please specify______________________________

(12) When the label *educational* is used, what image of your fellow students and teacher comes to mind?
- ❑ The students are competitors and the teacher is an authority figure.
- ❑ The students are colleagues and the teacher is a facilitator of learning.
- ❑ The students are a resource.
- ❑ The teacher is a resource.
- ❑ Other: Please specify______________________________

(13) In which setting would you learn best?
- ❑ A formal setting that is highly structured.
- ❑ An informal setting where exploration can take place individually or collectively.
- ❑ Other: Please specify______________________________

(14) In an educational setting, who should do the planning for the learning experience?
- ❑ The teacher.
- ❑ The students.
- ❑ Students *and* teacher through participative decision making (a collaborative process involving the students and teacher).
- ❑ Other: Please specify______________________________

(15) In an educational setting, who should determine the needs of those involved in the learning experience?
- ❑ The teacher.
- ❑ The students.
- ❑ Mutual assessment (both teacher and students).
- ❑ Other: Please specify____

(16) In an educational setting, who should set the goals to be achieved through the learning experience?
- ❑ The teacher.
- ❑ The students.
- ❑ Mutual negotiation (both teacher and students).
- ❑ Other: Please specify____

(17) Learning is more enjoyable for you when:
- ❑ The teacher plans what we will learn.
- ❑ The students plan what we will learn.
- ❑ The teacher and students agree upon and design a plan for learning.
- ❑ Other: Please specify____

(18) Learning is most enjoyable for me when:
- ❑ Teachers assign work for me to do.
- ❑ I engage in independent study.
- ❑ Other: Please specify____

(19) Who should evaluate a learning experience?
- ❑ The teacher.
- ❑ The students.
- ❑ Mutual assessment (both students and teacher).
- ❑ Other: Please specify____

(20) How important is the physical environment to the effectiveness of the learning experience (room size, types of furniture, accessibility)?
- ❑ Very important.
- ❑ Fairly important.
- ❑ Not important.
- ❑ Other: Please specify____

(21) Why do you participate in various learning experiences?
- ❑ To gather more information on a particular subject.
- ❑ For personal growth.
- ❑ Other: Please specify____

(22) How important is a learning atmosphere that affirms you and your self-worth?
- ❑ Very important
- ❑ Fairly important
- ❑ Not important
- ❑ Other: Please specify____

(23) I am more inclined to attend church school class when:
- ❑ It involves unchanging approaches.
- ❑ It involves changing, exploratory approaches.
- ❑ Other: Please specify________________________________

(24) Does your need to be liked and accepted affect your involvement in the church school?
- ❑ Yes
- ❑ No
- ❑ Other: Please specify________________________________

(25) Are you better motivated when your interests are addressed rather than predetermined by the teacher?
- ❑ My own interests.
- ❑ The interests of others.
- ❑ Other: Please specify________________________________

(26) As an adult, should Christian education address the various stages that adults go through in life, such as early adulthood, middle age, and later maturity?
- ❑ Yes
- ❑ No
- ❑ Other: Please specify________________________________

(27) What are the most important elements as you consider the climate for learning? (Rank them from 1 to 4.)
- ❑ The climate (temperature) of the room.
- ❑ The comfortableness of the chairs.
- ❑ The way a person is welcomed into a class by its members.
- ❑ The spirit of the whole church.

(28) What factors discourage you from continuing your involvement in the church school? (Rank them from 1 to 4.)
- ❑ Poor programs.
- ❑ Poor teacher preparation.
- ❑ Doesn't meet my needs.
- ❑ Doesn't address my interests.

(29) What effect do you feel the climate in our church has on your interest in Christian education? (Check only one response.)
- ❑ Enhances my interest.
- ❑ Lessens my interest.
- ❑ Other: Please specify________________________________

(30) Which statement best expresses your attitude about the relevance of Christian education for you?
- ❑ "I need to grow continually through Christian education."
- ❑ "I don't need to learn any more."
- ❑ "I've been in the church for years."

(31) Our church school and other Christian education opportunities are more important in helping to keep my faith strong than they are in helping to keep

our congregation strong. (Check only one response.)
❑ Strong disagreement
❑ Disagreement
❑ Mild disagreement
❑ Mild agreement
❑ Agreement
❑ Strong agreement

(32) It is more important for our church school and other Christian education opportunities to prepare me to serve others than it is to strengthen my personal faith. (Check only one response.)
❑ Strong disagreement
❑ Disagreement
❑ Mild disagreement
❑ Mild agreement
❑ Agreement
❑ Strong agreement

(33) The term *church school* does not necessarily mean "Sunday school"; what is the most convenient day or night and time for you to be involved in a church school class? (Please list.)

____

____

(34) How do you feel about the church school offering a choice of elective classes in which you could participate? (Check only one response.)
❑ Positive
❑ Negative
❑ Other: Please specify____________________________

(35) Please list your needs and share how the church school can assist in meeting those needs.

____

____

____

(36) Are you willing to pay a fee for resources (books, tapes, etc.) used in a church school learning setting? (Check only one response.)
❑ Yes
❑ No
❑ Other: Please specify____________________________

(37) What do you feel is the mission of Christian education?
❑ To produce knowledgeable Christian persons.
❑ To produce competent Christian persons.
❑ Other: Please specify____________________________

(38) What do you feel is the mission of a Christian teacher/educator?
❑ To operate "successful" educational activities (success is defined in terms of the numbers and enthusiasm of the participants).

- ❑ To help individuals satisfy their needs and achieve their goals.
- ❑ Other: Please specify________________________________

(39) Please identify which statement best sums up your opinion on Christian education:
- ❑ Learning is primarily a function of youth; Christian education supplies youth with all the knowledge they will need for the rest of their lives.
- ❑ Learning is a lifelong process.
- ❑ Other: Please specify________________________________

(40) Which definition best expresses your understanding of a "mature Christian person"?
- ❑ A mature Christian person is one who has attained a certain level of achievement.
- ❑ A mature Christian person is one who knows a large number of facts.
- ❑ A mature Christian person is one who grows in knowledge and the wise use of it.
- ❑ Other: Please specify________________________________

(41) How do you view the learning process?
- ❑ Learning is active—we are active inquirers after knowledge.
- ❑ Learning is passive—we are passive recipients of knowledge.
- ❑ Other: Please specify________________________________

(42) Which statement best describes your conception of a Christian educator/teacher?
- ❑ Someone who educates and transmits knowledge to others, telling them what they ought to know.
- ❑ Someone who facilitates the learning process, is a "change agent," and performs a "helping role."
- ❑ Other: Please specify________________________________

(43) Which list of terms best describes your understanding of the role of a Christian educator/teacher?
- ❑ Helper, guide, encourager, consultant, resource
- ❑ Transmitter, disciplinarian, judge, authority
- ❑ Other: Please specify________________________________

(44) Which statement best describes your previous experience with school (both secular school and church school)?
- ❑ "I wasn't smart in school."
- ❑ "I was treated with disrespect and greatly feared failure."
- ❑ "I was treated with respect and felt that I could succeed."
- ❑ Other: Please specify________________________________

(45) Which setting makes you feel more "adult"?
- ❑ An atmosphere that is formal and impersonal with status distinction between teacher and students.
- ❑ An atmosphere that is informal and friendly, where you are known by name and valued as a unique individual.
- ❑ Other: Please specify________________________________

(46) Please indicate where the following terms represent positive or negative feelings toward education: (Check only one.)

	Pos.	Neg.
(a) School building	❑	❑
(b) Podium on a stage	❑	❑
(c) Chairs placed in a row	❑	❑
(d) Chalkboards	❑	❑
(e) Chairs placed in a circle	❑	❑
(f) Small, informal learning groups	❑	❑

(47) Which behavior best conveys your expectation of a Christian educator/teacher? (Rank them 1 to 4.)

❑ A teacher should know me individually (by name).
❑ A teacher should show interest in me and respect toward me.
❑ A teacher should listen to what I have to say.
❑ A teacher should show that he or she really cares about me.

(48) Do you view learning as "proactive" or "reactive"?

❑ Learning is reactive—I react to information transmitted via books, lectures, etc.
❑ Learning is proactive—It is a self-directed personal learning style.

(49) As educational activities are planned, under what circumstances are you inclined to be more committed?

❑ I feel more committed to an activity when an educator/teacher makes necessary decisions.
❑ I feel more committed to an activity when I have participated in making it (or planning it).
❑ Other: Please specify______________________________

(50) Do you view personal experience as being of value and relevant to the learning experience?

❑ Yes
❑ No
❑ Other: Please specify______________________________

(51) Are you presently participating in the church school program as a learner?

❑ Yes
❑ No

(52) Were you a former participant in the church school program as a learner?

❑ Yes
❑ No

(53) How old are you?

❑ 18-29	❑ 60-69
❑ 30-39	❑ 70-79
❑ 40-49	❑ 80-89
❑ 50-59	

(54) Are you:

❑ Male ❑ Female

EXPLANATORY NOTES

Question 1 - The earliest experiences of persons in the church school setting often determine their willingness (or unwillingness) to participate in church school or other learning settings.

Question 2 - Choices 1 and 2 address the concept of modeling, which is more in line with an andragogical approach to learning, while choice 3 is derived from a pedagogical approach to learning.

Question 3 - James J. Deboy, Jr. asserts that if school means "fear of being called on" and "memorizing," then someone who associates adult religious education with his or her experience of schooling will avoid religious education because "the speaker might call on me" (taken from *Getting Started in Adult Religious Education*).

Question 4 - Choices 1 and 3 are from a pedagogical perspective; choice 2 reflects an andragogical perspective.

Question 5 - This question assesses the opinion of the congregation regarding our church school and its effectiveness.

Question 6 - Malcolm Knowles asserts that under the pedagogical approach to teaching and learning, the concept of the learner is that of a dependent personality. When the andragogical approach to teaching and learning is used, the concept of the learner moves toward an increasing self-direction.

Question 7 - Pedagogy views the role of the learners' experience as something to be built on more than used, while andragogy views the role of the learners' experience as a rich resource for learning. Knowles believes that when adults feel their experience isn't valuable and relevant to the learning experience, they feel rejected.

Question 8 - Knowles asserts that the success of learning under the pedagogical approach depends upon the level of maturity possessed by the individual approaching the learning task. Andragogy, however, holds that the readiness of persons to learn develops from life tasks and problems.

Question 9 - Pedagogy approaches the learning task from a subject-centered perspective while andragogy is task- or problem-centered.

Question 10 - Pedagogy asserts that persons are made to learn by external rewards and punishments, while andragogy asserts that persons are motivated to learn by internal incentives and curiosity.

Question 11 - The pedagogical approach asserts that most persons approach learning with the belief that they will apply what they've learned at a later time (postponed application). The andragogical approach, because it is task- or problem-centered, believes in the immediacy of application in learning.

Question 12 - The pedagogical approach to learning is formal, authority-oriented, competitive, and judgmental, while the andragogical approach to learning is informal, mutually respectful, consensual, collaborative, and supportive.

Question 13 - This question attempts to ascertain whether a formal setting (pedagogical) or an informal setting (andragogical) is the most desirable.

Question 14 - In the pedagogical learning model, the teacher does the planning; in the andragogical learning model, participative decision making (a collaborative process involving the students and teacher) is used.

Question 15 - In the pedagogical learning model, the teacher assesses the needs; in the andragogical learning model, needs are determined by mutual assessment.

Question 16 - In the pedagogical learning model, the teacher sets the goals; in the andragogical learning model, goals are set by mutual negotiation.

Question 17 - Choice 1 reflects the pedagogical model for learning; choice 3 reflects the andragogical model.

Question 18 - Pedagogy adheres to transmittal techniques and assigned readings, while andragogy adheres more to inquiry projects, independent study, and experimental techniques.

Question 19 - In the pedagogical learning model, evaluation is primarily by the teacher, whereas in the andragogical learning model, evaluation occurs by mutual assessment.

Question 20 - Malcolm Knowles says that physical needs largely determine the willingness (or unwillingness) of adults to participate in the learning experience (physical needs).

Question 21 - Choice 1 is an appropriate response for one who is most comfortable with the pedagogical learning model, while choice 2 is suitable for those who are concerned with the fundamental urge to keep growing as a person (growth needs).

Question 22 - Self-respect and self-worth are paramount needs for adults. When these needs are not respected or are violated, some react by withdrawing into a shell, and others try to protect themselves by dominating or controlling the situation.

Question 23 - Persons tend to get excited about learning experiences that are different, as opposed to the same traditional mode of learning.

Question 24 - See explanatory notes, Question 22.

Question 25 - James J. Deboy, Jr. says that adult religious education should be based on real needs and interests, both individual and communal, and the interests of the participants. To do this, a serious effort must be made to determine these needs and interests.

Question 26 - Adult education needs to address the theory found in the thought of Erik Erikson (Eight Ages), Bernard Doelen (Developmental Theory), and Roger Gould.

Question 27 - James J. Deboy, Jr. says the learning climate includes the physical room and the comfortableness of the chairs. The climate includes how people are welcomed as they enter and thanked as they leave. The learning climate includes the spirit of the whole parish.

Question 28 - James J. Deboy, Jr. says that poor programs are probably the biggest factor in discouraging people from continuing their religious learning.

Question 29 - Assessment of the "climate" of our congregation.

Question 30 - James J. Deboy, Jr. says that too many people in the church somehow have gotten the idea (perhaps it was learned in some of the educational programs in which they participated) that they can't learn any more ("you can't teach an old dog new tricks") or they don't need to learn any more. Such attitudes are among the most serious obstacles to developing a program of adult religious education.

Question 31 - This question addresses the function of church school and Christian education. Do persons see the teaching ministry of the church as more beneficial to their personal faith or to the overall strength of the congregation?

Question 32 - This question also addresses the function of church school and Christian education. Do persons see the teaching ministry of the church as preparation for serving others or more beneficial to their personal faith?

Questions 33-36 - These questions are for the purpose of needs assessment.

Question 37 - Malcolm Knowles says that the mission of education is to produce competent people—this is the andragogical approach to learning. The pedagogical approach to learning says that the mission of education is to produce knowledgeable people.

Question 38 - Choice 1 adheres to the pedagogical approach to learning, while choice 2 adheres to the andragogical approach.

Question 39 - Choice 1 adheres to the pedagogical approach to learning, while choice 2 adheres to the andragogical approach. Most adults alive today were educated in their youth according to the doctrine that learning is primarily a function of youth.

Question 40 - A person's understanding of what "mature" means will largely determine whether or not he/she feels that education ended at youth or is a life-long process.

Question 41 - Is learning an active or passive process? Is a student "a plant to be nurtured" or "a jug to be filled"? This question examines whether one is a passive recipient of knowledge or an active inquirer after knowledge.

Questions 42-43 - A person's concept of the function of a teacher helps determine whether he/she is most comfortable with a pedagogical or andragogical approach to learning.

Question 44 - Malcolm Knowles says that adults often carry over from their previous experience with schooling the perception that they are not very smart, at least with regard to academic work. When adults remember the classroom as a place where they were treated with disrespect and feared failure, this creates a serious barrier to their becoming involved in adult education activities at all.

Question 45 - People tend to feel more "adult" in a friendly, informal atmosphere where they are known by name and valued as unique individuals, rather than in the traditional school atmosphere of formality, semi-anonymity, and status differentiation between teacher and student.

Question 46 - Items 1, 2, 3, and 4 are all consistent with a pedagogical approach to learning, while items 5 and 6 are consistent with an andragogical approach to learning. Items 1, 2, 3, and 4 represent symbols of childishness to particular groups of adults, while items 5 and 6 represent a more "adult" symbol of learning.

Question 47 - The behavior of a teacher probably influences the character of the learning climate more than any other single factor.

Question 48 - See explanatory notes, Question 41.

Question 49 - See explanatory notes, Question 14.

Question 50 - See explanatory notes, Question 7.

Questions 51-52 - These questions are asked to determine the extent of a person's involvement in the church school, either present or past.

Questions 53-54 - These questions attempt to establish whether there is a connection among age, sex, and involvement (or lack of involvement) in the church school.

APPENDIX B

EVALUATION OF CHURCH SCHOOL TEACHER TRAINING SESSION

Topic: Date:______________________

Scripture:

Circle the phrase that best describes your reaction to the presentation:

1. How effective is the instructor in communicating information and ideas?

   not at all   a little   somewhat   quite a bit   extremely

2. Was the information that was communicated deemed valuable to the individual student-teachers?

   not at all   a little   somewhat   quite a bit   extremely

3. How effective is the instructor in communicating goals to individual student-teachers?

   not at all   a little   somewhat   quite a bit   extremely

4. Are these goals attainable?

   not at all   a little   somewhat   quite a bit   extremely

5. Was the teaching model used by the instructor appropriate?

   not at all   a little   somewhat   quite a bit   extremely

6. Were the teaching materials used by the instructor difficult?

   not at all   a little   somewhat   quite a bit   extremely

7. Is the instructor open to ideas or opinions other than his/her own? To what degree?

   not at all   a little   somewhat   quite a bit   extremely

EVALUATION OF CHURCH SCHOOL TEACHER

Topic: Date:____________________

Scripture:

Read the following statements, then circle the phrase that best describes your reaction to the teacher's presentation:

1. During this presentation I learned:

   nothing new a little some quite a lot a great deal

2. Opportunity for class participation was:

   not at all a little somewhat quite a bit extremely

3. My interest in the subject matter has been increased:

   not at all a little somewhat quite a bit a great deal

4. To what degree is the teacher's expectancy for each student's growth clearly evident?

   not at all somewhat average a great deal

5. How open is the teacher to the use of various teaching models?

   not at all a little somewhat quite a bit completely open

6. Does the teacher's presentation demonstrate that adequate preparation and research have occurred?

   not at all somewhat quite a bit a great deal

7. Is the teacher's enthusiasm for the subject matter indicative of his or her commitment to the principles taught?

   not at all somewhat quite a bit a great deal

8. Does the teacher demonstrate sensitivity to the varying levels of understanding among those he or she teaches?

   not at all a little somewhat quite a bit a great deal

Comments:

Overall performance of the teacher:

Appendix C
Lesson Preparation

Date_______________ Text_________________ Title______________

Keyword:

Proposition:

Factual Data and Background Material:
Sequence of Events: (what happened? when? in what order?)

People Involved: (who? what is their significance?)

Places Involved: (where? what is the significance?)

Questions/Concerns/Problems that might arise during discussion:

Theological truth for living: (arises out of factual data)

TEACHING PLAN

Date____________________ Scripture Text(s)___________________________

My AIM for this session is to help the learners with:

Body Life: (getting acquainted, body building, acceptance, affection)
Learning Activity:

Time Required:
Materials Required:

Study of the Scripture:
Introduce the Subject: (hook the interest of the group)
Learning Activity:

Time Required:
Materials Required:

Study the Text:
Learning Activity:

Time Required:
Materials Required:

Life Response: (application of the scripture to life)
Learning Activity:

Time Required:
Materials Required:

THE TEACHING PLAN – AN EFFECTIVE, ACTIVITY-ORIENTED APPROACH TO TEACHING THE CHURCH SCHOOL LESSON

LESSON PREPARATION

TEXT: List the appropriate scripture text(s) you will use in the course of the lesson.

TITLE: Select a title that includes a keyword and that reflects the central theme of the lesson.

PROPOSITION: This simple statement should reflect the point you are attempting to prove in the lesson. For example, if you are teaching a lesson on forgiveness, a possible proposition would be: *Forgiveness is promised to every Christian.*

SEQUENCE OF EVENTS: Look at the events in the scripture and organize them into their logical progression. Understanding the order of events helps the teacher have a clear understanding of the story as it occurred in the scripture. Thus, your approach to teaching the lesson can take on a story form (especially if you are teaching young children or teenagers).

PEOPLE INVOLVED: Gather information on all persons who appear in the course of the scripture lesson. This is accomplished most effectively through consulting Bible dictionaries and other resources that give needed information on those characters.

PLACES INVOLVED: In many lessons that you will be required to teach, there are geographical locations that are highly significant. For example, if you are teaching a lesson on Jesus' triumphal entry into Jerusalem, you will need to examine the biblical importance of the city and even the present-day significance of the city.

PROBLEMS/CONCERNS/QUESTIONS: Think of possible questions class members may raise, as well as any textual difficulties that may arise. For example, if difficult scripture passages are a part of the lesson, be prepared to deal with them (e.g., the difficult sayings of Jesus).

THEOLOGICAL TRUTHS FOR LIVING: Make a list of every biblical/theological truth that arises out of the text (e.g., the love of God, the grace of God, etc.).

TEACHING PLAN

THE LESSON AIM: The lesson aim should express in succinct terms what you intend to accomplish, including the keyword you identified in your preparation.

BODY LIFE: (1 Cor. 12:27 BUILDING COMMUNITY WITHIN THE CHURCH SCHOOL CLASS) This activity should encourage interaction among class members. If we are to experience *koinonia* as it is meant to occur within the Body of Christ, we must take some intentional steps to facilitate such a wholesome, Christian environment. The key to the Body Life activity is to help Christians interact.

BIBLE STUDY: (A DIET OF FRESH INSIGHTS FROM SCRIPTURE) This portion of the lesson calls for the teacher to examine the biblical record with the class. The traditional approach usually takes the form of reading directly from the scriptures. Creativity, however, can be exercised in dealing with the given biblical account. For example, storytelling can be used very effectively with all audiences, especially younger audiences.

FEEL FREE TO USE YOUR IMAGINATION AND CREATIVITY! Include an activity that causes the class to look closely at the biblical account (also include the materials you will need).

LIFE RESPONSE: This activity helps the persons in the class to appropriate the truths of the scripture to their lives. The student should arise with a sense of how the Word of God is relevant to his or her life situation. The commitment activity should express in practical terms a method by which the student can live out the truth of the scripture.

SAMPLE LESSON

Text: Luke 7:36-50 Title: FORGIVENESS IS GREAT

Keyword: Forgiveness

Proposition: It is wonderful to be forgiven.

Factual Data and Background Material:
(with theological truth for living identified)

Sequence of events:

1. Jesus eats at the home of Simon.

He must have been a much sought-after guest (11:37; 14:1).
Open to all (vs. 33-39).

2. The woman washes and anoints Jesus' feet.

Illustrates the deep sensitivity of troubled people. Intent in her search.

3. Simon criticizes Jesus.

Beware of jumping to conclusions.

4. Jesus replies with a parable.

"Cool," not defensive. Man is a hopeless debtor who can't repay.

5. Jesus pronounces the woman forgiven.

It's great to be clean, fresh.

People involved:

1. **Jesus**—guest of Simon (cf. vs. 34).

Open to all:

Eats with Simon

Receives worship

Pronounces forgiveness

2. **Simon**—A Pharisee, a strict religionist. Invited, hosted, criticized.

Narrowness blocks our view. Impressions are often a poor foundation for judgment.

Dismissed the woman as beneath him.

Our bias colors our perception.

Deluded, his debt not great.

3. **The woman**—Sinner, ritually impure, perhaps a prostitute (vs. 39, 47).

Weeping.

Emotions express deep feelings.

Wiping, anointing, kissing (worshiping). Accepted (vs. 44). Forgiven.

Real worship costs the worshiper.

4. **Those at table** (hostile, questioning).

Our attitude limits what we can receive.

Places involved:

Nain (vs. 11)?

House of Simon

The Bible gives an important place to table fellowship.

Problems:

1. Why would Jesus eat with a Pharisee? Christians must be open.
2. What does the parable mean?
3. What is the relationship between forgiveness and love?

TEACHING PLAN

Date____________________ Scripture________________________

AIM: To help my class understand that forgiveness is promised to every Christian

BODY LIFE: (a warm and accepting climate, introduce a subject)

Activity: Find a partner and share:

1. Favorite game at age nine
2. A problem I faced as a child and how I worked it out.

Create groups of four by joining two groups:

1. Introduce your partner to the group
2. Prepare a list of biblical persons who experienced forgiveness

Share lists on overhead

Materials Needed: Overhead, transparencies, markers

BIBLE STUDY: (a diet of fresh insights from scripture)

Input: 1. Read Luke 7:36-40 Time: 24 min.

2. Share outline: (overhead)

   I. The Woman Found Forgiveness

   II. Simon Ignored Forgiveness

   III. Jesus Provides Forgiveness

Activity:

1. Half the groups compile a list of the characteristics of the woman. The other half compiles a list of the characteristics of Simon.
2. From these lists, compile a chart on the overhead comparing the woman and Simon.

Materials Needed: Overhead, transparency, pencils, paper

LIFE RESPONSE:

Self-Evaluation Activity:

1. Prepare a graph comparing the experiences of forgiveness of:

(little) 1 2 3 4 5 6 7 (much)

Simon	####
Woman	###################
Jesus	###################
You	##########

Commitment Activity:

2. Write a memo to yourself about what you could do to improve your reception of or offering of forgiveness in the next week.

Materials Needed: Chart on 3 x 5 card, pencils, paper

APPENDIX D

CONGREGATIONAL SURVEY FOR CONTEXTUAL ASSESSMENT

This survey is helpful in understanding the demographics of a congregation (age, sex, marital status, education, income, etc.). It is also helpful in assessing pastoral leadership needs, worship preferences, and fellowship needs. In addition, it informs the teachers' ability to plan and develop teaching strategies that are appropriate to the varied educational levels within the congregation. The author suggests administering this survey on an annual basis because of the changing needs of your congregation.

1. ❑ Male ❑ Female
2. Age:
3. Are you:
   ❑ Single/never married ❑ Married ❑ Widowed ❑ Separated/divorced
4. Do you have children?
   ❑ No children ❑ infant to 12 years ❑ 13-18 years ❑ 19 years and older
5. What is the highest level of education you have completed?
   ❑ Elementary school ❑ Some high school ❑ Graduated from high school
   ❑ Some college ❑ Graduated from college ❑ Postgraduate work
6. Occupation: ______________________________
7. In which school district do you reside?
8. How long have you lived there?
9. What is your annual family income?
   ❑ Less than $10,000 ❑ $10,000 to $14,999 ❑ $15,000 to $19,999
   ❑ $20,000 to $29,999 ❑ $30,000 to $39,999 ❑ $40,000 to $49,999
   ❑ $50,000 to $59,999 ❑ $60,000 to $74,999 ❑ $75,000 to $99,999
   ❑ Over $100,000
10. Name of denomination/church affiliation in which you grew up?
11. How long have you been a member of *(Name)* United Methodist Church?
12. How often do you attend on average?
    ❑ Less than once a month ❑ 1 out of 4 Sundays per month
    ❑ 2 out of 4 Sundays per month ❑ 3 out of 4 Sundays per month
    ❑ 4 out of 4 Sundays per month
13. What activities/organizations/groups are you involved in in your community?

PASTOR AND PASTORAL LEADERSHIP

14. If the pastor of *(Name)* United Methodist Church were of the following racial backgrounds, would it be a problem, an asset, or make no difference to you?

	Problem	Asset	No difference
Asian			
Black			
Hispanic			
White			
Other (specify)			

15. Rank the top three (3) following worship and preaching styles according to your preference:
❑ Fire-and-brimstone ❑ Evangelistic ❑ Abstract, philosophical, intellectual
❑ Psychological ❑ Political-social
❑ Biblical but related to daily life, personal
❑ Other (specify):

16. Rank the top three (3) most important activities of the pastor:
❑ Administration ❑ Relational skills and interaction with people
❑ Evangelism and outreach ❑ Ministry to the elderly
❑ Visitation and counseling ❑ Preaching and worship leadership
❑ Stewardship and finances ❑ Education, teaching
❑ Mission emphasis and awareness

WORSHIP

17. Which style of music do you prefer in the worship service?
(Strongly like) 1 2 3 4 5 (Strongly dislike)

Traditional hymns	1 2 3 4 5
Classical/sacred	1 2 3 4 5
Contemporary Christian	1 2 3 4 5
Gospel	1 2 3 4 5
Christian Rock	1 2 3 4 5
Other (specify):	1 2 3 4 5

18. Do you generally like the following forms of participation in the worship service?

	Yes	No
Clapping	❑	❑
Spontaneous amens	❑	❑
Unison, printed prayers and responses	❑	❑
Sharing of concerns and celebrations	❑	❑
Other (specify):	❑	❑

19. I wish the church's worship style were:
❑ More formal ❑ Same ❑ Less formal

20. How did you come to this church?
❑ Through family who were already members
❑ Through friends who are already members
❑ Live or lived in the neighborhood of the church
❑ Heard about the church from someone
❑ Other (specify):

21. What do you prefer in terms of the time frame of the worship service?
❑ Under 1 hour ❑ About 1 hour
❑ Up to 1 hour 15 minutes ❑ Up to 1 hour 30 minutes
❑ Over 1 hour 30 minutes

FELLOWSHIP

22. Which groups do you attend and participate in at the church? Please specify.
    - ❑ Committees:
    - ❑ Sunday school classes:
    - ❑ Bible study:
    - ❑ Short-term, evening study groups:
    - ❑ Choirs:
    - ❑ Informal gatherings (picnics, potlucks, etc.):

23. Given an interest in a group in the church, do you feel that you could freely join any of them? If not, why?

	Yes	No
Committees	❑	❑
Sunday school classes	❑	❑
Bible study	❑	❑
Short-term, evening study groups	❑	❑
Choirs	❑	❑
Informal gatherings (potlucks, etc.)	❑	❑

Any comments:

24. What makes you decide to attend or participate in a social gathering?
    ❑ Long-term commitment to it ❑ Interest ❑ Invitation of friend or member

25. Which two (2) factors attract you the most to this church?
    - ❑ Worship service ❑ The pastor
    - ❑ Location of the church ❑ The diversity of the congregation
    - ❑ Program (activities, Sunday school, mission projects, etc.)
    - ❑ The people in the congregation (personalities, friends)
    - ❑ Other (specify):

26. How do you feel about racial change and a mixed congregation?
    - ❑ Doesn't matter one way or the other to me
    - ❑ Uncomfortable initially but could accept this change
    - ❑ Uncomfortable and wouldn't accept this change

27. If the church's racial mix became predominantly white, would you feel:
    - ❑ Uncomfortable and leave ❑ Uncomfortable but stay
    - ❑ Okay about it ❑ Pleased
    - ❑ Other (specify):

28. What do you think the church's direction should be?
    - ❑ Not to pay any attention to racial mix
    - ❑ Encourage white families to join
    - ❑ Other (specify).

A special note of thanks to Dr. Sally Dyck for the development and use of this survey.

BIBLIOGRAPHY

Foundations for Teaching and Learning in The United Methodist Church. Nashville: Discipleship Resources, 1979. Out of print.

Foundations: Shaping the Ministry of Christian Education in Your Congregation. Nashville: Discipleship Resources, 1993.

"Return to Spiritual Traditions of Black Churches and Schools." *Ebony* (August 1986).

"Sunday School May Keep Your Kids Out of Jail, Study." *Jet* (December 22, 1986).

"The Black Church and the Sunday School Movement." *The Church School Herald-Journal 66,* No. 2 (December, January, February 1980-81).

The Book of Discipline of The United Methodist Church, 1976. Nashville: The United Methodist Publishing House, 1976.

Alessi, Vincie. *Evangelism in Your Church School.* Valley Forge, PA: Judson Press, 1978.

Allison, Dr. Richard E. *Teaching Plan.* CE 511 Educational Ministries. Ashland Theological Seminary, Fall, 1985, in Ashland, Ohio.

Allison, Dr. Richard E. "Adult Ministry." Lectures delivered at Ashland Theological Seminary, March 9-May 22, 1987, in Ashland, Ohio.

Anderson, David W. and Brooker, Wendell. *Expanding Your Church School Program.* Valley Forge, PA: Judson Press, 1983.

Bennett, G. Willis. *Guidelines for Effective Urban Church Ministry.* Nashville: Broadman Press, 1983.

Benson, Warren S. and Gangel, Kenneth O. *Christian Education: Its History and Philosophy.* Chicago: Moody Press, 1983.

Billingsley, Andrew. *Black Families and the Struggle for Survival.* New York: Friendship Press, 1974.

Braden, Suzanne G. *Evangelism Ministries Planning Handbook.* Nashville: Discipleship Resources, 1987.

Brantley, William. *I Can Plan for Children's Ministries.* Nashville: Discipleship Resources, 1979. Out of print.

Brown, Lowell E. *Your Sunday School Can Grow.* Glendale: Gospel Light Publications, 1974.

Callahan, Kennon L. *Twelve Keys to an Effective Church.* New York: Harper and Row, 1983.

Campbell, Ross. *How to Really Love Your Child.* Wheaton, IL: Scripture Press, 1979.

Chartier, Jan. *Developing Leadership in the Teaching Church.* Valley Forge, PA: Judson Press, 1985.

Coffin, Henry Sloane and Mullenburg, James. "The Book of Isaiah," *The Interpreter's Bible,* Vol. 5. Nashville: Abingdon-Cokesbury Press, 1951.

Coleman, Caesar D. ed. *Beyond Blackness to Destiny.* No publisher, no date.

Cone, James H. *Black Theology and Black Power.* New York: The Seabury Press, 1969.

_______. *For My People.* Maryknoll: Orbis Books, 1984.

_______. *The Theology of Liberation.* Philadelphia: Lippincott, 1970.

DeBoy, James J. *Getting Started in Adult Religious Education.* New York: Paulist Press, 1979.

Drushal, Dr. Mary Ellen. "Children's Ministry." Lecture delivered at Ashland Theological Seminary, March 8-May 21, 1986, Ashland, Ohio.

Dyck, Sally. From unpublished work, "On Earth as It Is in Heaven: The Characteristics of a Racially Inclusive Church."

Elias, John C. *The Foundations and Practice of Adult Religious Education.* Malabar, FL: Robert E. Krieger Publishing Company, 1982.

Everist, Norma J. *Education Ministry in the Congregation.* Minneapolis: Augsburg Publishing House, 1983.

Ewers, Duane A. *Do You Care? Compassion in the Sunday School.* Nashville: Discipleship Resources, 1987.

Felkner, Myrtle. *Making the Church School Better.* Nashville: Discipleship Resources, 1980.

Foster, Charles R. *Teaching in the Community of Faith.* Nashville: Abingdon Press, 1982.

Foster, Charles R., Johnson, Ethel R., and Shockley, Grant S. *Christian Education Journey of Black Americans—Past, Present, Future.* Nashville: Discipleship Resources, 1985. Out of print.

Frazier, E. Franklin. *The Negro Church in America.* New York: Schocken Books, 1973.

Freire, Paulo. *Pedagogy of the Oppressed.* New York: The Seabury Press, 1972.

Friedenberg, Edgar Z. *The Vanishing Adolescent.* New York: Dell Publications, 1959.

Furnish, Dorothy Jean. *Exploring the Bible with Children.* Nashville: Abingdon Press, 1975.

Goodwin, Bennie E. II. *The Effective Teacher—A Christian's Guide to Teaching.* Downers Grove: InterVarsity Press, 1985.

Graendorf, Werner C. "Materials for Working with Youth," Roy Zuck and Warren S. Bensen, eds. *Youth Education in the Church.* Chicago: Moody Press, 1978.

Hale-Benson, Janice E. *Black Children—Their Roots, Culture, and Learning Styles.* Baltimore: The Johns Hopkins University Press, 1986.

Hance, Eleanor and Richard Troup. "Materials for Working with Youth," Roy B. Zuck and Roy G. Irving, eds. *Youth and the Church.* Chicago: Moody Press, 1968.

Harner, Nevin C. *Youth Work in the Church.* Nashville: Abingdon Press, n.d.

Hartman, Warren J. *A Study of the Church School in The United Methodist Church.* Nashville: Discipleship Resources, 1976. Out of print.

Hawkins, Thomas R. *Building God's People.* Nashville: Discipleship Resources, 1990.

Hendricks, Howard C. *Teaching to Change Lives.* Portland, OR: Multnomah Press, 1987.

Hester, H. I. *The Heart of Hebrew History.* Liberty, MO: Quality Press, Inc., 1962.

Hinson, William H. *A Place to Dig in—Doing Evangelism in the Local Church.* Nashville: Abingdon Press, 1987.

Hoeldtke, Clyde and Lawrence O. Richards. *A Theology of Church Leadership.* Grand Rapids: Zondervan Publishing House, 1980.

Hoglund, Gunnar. *Success Handbook for Youth Groups.* Chicago: Harvest Publications, 1978.

Jones, Major J. *Black Awareness—A Theology of Hope.* Nashville: Abingdon Press, 1971.

Kishpaugh, Charles. *Friends in Faith: Mentoring Youth in the Church.* Nashville: Discipleship Resources, 1994.

Knowles, Malcolm S. *The Modern Practice of Adult Education.* Englewood Cliffs, N.J.: The Adult Education Company, n.d.

_______. *Self-Directed Learning.* New York: The Adult Education Company, 1975.

Krau, Carol, ed. *Planning for Christian Education.* Nashville: Discipleship Resources, 1994.

Kunjufu, Jawanza. *Countering the Conspiracy to Destroy Black Boys.* Chicago: African American Images, 1985.

Lee, James Michael, ed. *The Religious Education We Need.* Mishawaka: Religious Education Press, 1977.

Magness, Lee. "Teaching and Learning in the Gospels: The Biblical Basis of Christian Education," *Religious Education 70,* no. 6 (November-December, 1975).

Massey, Floyd Jr. and McKinney, Samuel Berry. *Church Administration in the Black Perspective.* Valley Forge, PA: Judson Press, 1976.

McClain, William B. *Black People in the Methodist Church—Whither Thou Goest?* Cambridge: Schenkman Publishing Company, 1984.

McCray, Walter Arthur. *Reaching and Teaching Black Young Adults.* Chicago: Black Light Fellowship, 1986.

Miles, Delos. *Introduction to Evangelism.* Nashville: Broadman Press, 1983.

Mitchell, Henry H. *Black Preaching.* San Francisco: Harper & Row, 1979.

_______. *Soul Theology.* San Francisco: Harper & Row, 1986.

Myers, William H. *God's Yes Was Louder Than My No—Rethinking the African American Call to Ministry.* Grand Rapids, MI: William B. Eerdmans Publishing Company, 1994.

Norton, MaryJane Pierce. *Teaching Young Children—A Guide for Teachers and Leaders.* Nashville: Discipleship Resources, 1989.

Norwood, Frederick A. *The Story of American Methodism.* Nashville: Abingdon Press, 1974.

Parks, Sharon. *The Critical Years: The Young Adult Search for a Faith to Live By.* San Francisco: Harper & Row, 1986.

Peterson, Gilbert A., ed. *The Christian Education of Adults.* Chicago: Moody Press, 1984.

Piland, Harry. *Basic Sunday School Work.* Nashville: Convention Press, 1980.

Pillow, Wright and Youngblood, Jennie. *The Church School of Few Members.* Nashville: Discipleship Resources, 1977. Out of print.

Richards, Lawrence O. *Youth Ministry: Its Renewal in the Local Church.* Grand Rapids, MI: Zondervan Publishing House, 1972.

_______. *A Theology of Christian Education.* Grand Rapids, MI: Zondervan Publishing House, 1975.

_______. *A Theology of Personal Ministry: Spiritual Giftedness in the Local Church.* Grand Rapids, MI: Zondervan Publishing House, 1981.

_______. *A Theology of Children's Ministry.* Grand Rapids, MI: Zondervan, 1983.

Richardson, G. "Developing a Unified Approach to Youth Ministry," G. Dausey, ed. *The Youth Leader's Source Book.* Grand Rapids, MI: Zondervan Publishing House, 1983.

Rogers, Donald B. *In Praise of Learning.* Nashville: Abingdon Press, 1980.

Runk, Lois M. *Working with Elementary Children—A Guide for Teachers and Leaders.* Nashville: Discipleship Resources, 1988. Out of print.

Ryan, Roy H., ed. *Christian Education Planning Handbook.* Nashville: Discipleship Resources, 1988. Out of print.

_______. *Invitational Teaching—Your Witness as a Sunday School Teacher.* Nashville: Discipleship Resources, 1988. Out of print.

Schaller, Lyle E. *Activating the Passive Church—Diagnosis and Treatment.* Nashville: Abingdon Press, 1981.

Seibert, Ronna. *Guidelines for Leading Your Church: 1993-1996— Adult Ministries.* Nashville: Abingdon Press, 1992.

Seymour, Jack L. *Contemporary Approaches to Christian Education.* Nashville: Abingdon Press, 1983.

Sherrill, Lewis Joseph. *The Rise of Christian Education.* New York: The Macmillan Company, 1944.

Shipley, Anthony J. "Resources in the Black Church." Nashville: General Board of Discipleship, The United Methodist Church, 1973. Out of print.

Skinner, Tom. *Black and Free.* Grand Rapids: Zondervan, 1968.

Smith, Glenn C., ed. *Evangelizing Blacks.* Wheaton, IL: Tyndale House Publishers, Inc., 1988.

Smith, J. Alfred, ed. *The Church in Bold Mission: A Guidebook on Black Church Development.* Atlanta: Department of Cooperative Ministries with National Baptists Home Mission Board, SBC, 1977.

Smith, Sid. *10 Super Sunday Schools in the Black Community.* Nashville: Broadman Press, 1986.

_____. *Reaching the Black Community Through the Sunday School.* Nashville: Convention Press, 1984.

Smith, Wallace Charles. *The Church in the Life of the Black Family.* Valley Forge: Judson Press, 1985.

Stallings, James O. *Telling the Story—Evangelism in Black Churches.* Valley Forge, PA: Judson Press, 1988.

Stewart, Carlyle Fielding III. *African American Church Growth—12 Principles for Prophetic Ministry.* Nashville: Abingdon Press, 1994.

Stokes, Kenneth, ed. *Faith Development in the Adult Life Cycle.* New York: W. H. Sadler, 1983.

Taylor, Marvin J., ed. *Changing Patterns of Religious Education.* Nashville: Abingdon Press, 1984.

Thomas, Dr. James S. "Doctor of Ministry Regional Seminar Lecture." Session conducted at United Theological Seminary, February 19-20, 1989, in Dayton, Ohio.

Tidwell, Charles A. *Educational Ministry of a Church.* Nashville: Broadman Press, 1982.

Tillich, Paul. *The Protestant Era.* Chicago: University of Chicago Press, Phoenix Books, 1957.

Ulich, Robert. *A History of Religious Education.* New York: New York University Press, 1968.

Vogel, Linda J. *Teaching Older Adults.* Nashville: Discipleship Resources, 1989. Out of print.

Washington, James M., ed. *A Testament of Hope—The Essential Writings of Martin Luther King, Jr.* San Francisco: Harper & Row, 1986.

Watley, William D. *Roots of Resistance—The Nonviolent Ethic of Martin Luther King, Jr.* Valley Forge, PA: Judson Press, 1985.

Westerhoff, John H. *Will Our Children Have Faith?* Minneapolis: The Winston-Seabury Press, 1976.

_______. *Living the Faith Community—The Church That Makes a Difference.* Minneapolis: Winston Press, Inc., 1985.

_______. *Building God's People.* New York: The Seabury Press, 1983.

_______. *Bringing Up Children in the Christian Faith.* Minneapolis: Winston Press, 1980.

Whitney, S. Leon. "Rediscovering the Foundation of Christian Education." Lecture delivered at the National Baptist Congress of Christian Education, June 22-26, 1981, in Omaha, Nebraska.

Wigginton, Eugene H. "Vital Signs of Leadership." *Key to Christian Education* (Spring 1986).

Wilhoit, Jim. *Christian Education—The Search for Meaning.* Grand Rapids, MI: Baker Book House, 1986.

Wilke, Richard B. *And Are We Yet Alive?—The Future of the United Methodist Church.* Nashville: Abingdon Press, 1986.

_______. *Signs and Wonders—The Mighty Work of God in the Church.* Nashville: Abingdon Press, 1989.

Williams, Willard A. *Resource Booklet: Educational Ministry in the Black Community.* Nashville: General Board of Discipleship,1972. Out of print.

Wyckoff, D. Campbell, ed. *Renewing the Sunday School and the CCD.* Birmingham: Religious Education Press, 1986.

ENDNOTES

1 Warren. J. Hartman, *A Study of the Church School in The United Methodist Church* (Nashville: Discipleship Resources, 1976), p. 21.

2 Floyd Massey, Jr. and Samuel Berry McKinney, *Church Administration in the Black Perspective* (Valley Forge, PA: Judson Press, 1976), p. 60.

3 Willard A. Williams, *Educational Ministry in the Black Community* (Nashville: Board of Education of The United Methodist Church, 1972), pp. 11-12.

4 James J. Deboy, Jr., *Getting Started in Adult Religious Education* (New York: Paulist Press, 1979), pp. 12-13.

5 Malcolm S. Knowles, *The Modern Practice of Adult Education* (Englewood Cliffs, N.J.: Cambridge, The Adult Education Company, n.d.), p. 40.

6 Ibid.

7 Ibid., pp. 42-43.

8 Ibid., p. 43.

9 Malcolm Knowles, *Self-Directed Learning* (New York: The Adult Education Company, 1975), p. 60.

10 Ibid.

11 Robert Ulich, *A History of Religious Education* (New York: New York University Press, 1968), p. 278.

12 Myrtle Felker, *Making the Church School Better* (Nashville: Discipleship Resources, 1980), pp. 21-22.

13 *Foundations: Shaping the Ministry of Christian Education in Your Congregation* (Nashville: Discipleship Resources, 1993), p. 24.

14 Charles R. Foster, Ethel R. Johnson, and Grant S. Shockley, *The Christian Education Journey of Black Americans—Past, Present, Future* (Nashville: Discipleship Resources, 1985), p. 20.

15 Ibid.

16 Ibid., p. 20

17 Ibid., p. 19.

18 Ibid., p. 20.

19 Ibid., p. 21.

20 Lewis Joseph Sherrill, *The Rise of Christian Education* (New York: The Macmillan Company, 1944), p. 21.

21 Ibid., p. 6.

22 Charles A. Tidwell, *Educational Ministry of a Church* (Nashville: Broadman Press, 1982), p. 18.

23 Ibid.

24 Ibid.

25 Ibid., p. 19.

26 Ibid.

27 Jawanza Kunjufu, *Countering the Conspiracy to Destroy Black Boys* (Chicago: African American Images, 1985), p. 27.

28 Sherrill, p. 13.

29 Tidwell, p. 21.

30 Ibid., p. 22.

31 Ibid.

32 H.I. Hester, *The Heart of Hebrew History* (Liberty, MO: The Quality Press, Inc., 1962), p. 169.

33 Ulich, p. 8.

34 Ibid., p. 21.

35 Sid Smith, *Reaching the Black Community Through the Sunday School* (Nashville: Convention Press, 1984), p. 146. Used by permission.

36 Warren S. Benson and Kenneth O. Gangel, *Christian Education: Its History and Philosophy* (Chicago: Moody Press, 1983), p. 69.

37 Lee Magness, "Teaching and Learning in the Gospels: The Biblical Basis of Christian Education," *Religious Education* 70, no. 6 (November-December, 1975): 629-35.

38 Tidwell, pp. 29-31.

39 Sid Smith, p. 146.

40 Clyde Hoeldtke and Lawrence O. Richards, *A Theology of Church Leadership* (Grand Rapids, MI: Zondervan Publishing House, 1980), p. 103.

41 James Mullenburg and Henry Sloane Coffin, "The Book of Isaiah," *The Interpreter's Bible*, Vol. 5 (Nashville: Abingdon-Cokesbury Press, 1951), p. 501.

42 Hoeldtke and Richards, p. 104.

43 Gib Martin and Lawrence O. Richards, *A Theology of Personal Ministry* (Grand Rapids: Zondervan Publishing House, 1981), p. 76.

44 Gilbert A. Peterson, *The Christian Education of Adults* (Chicago: Moody Press, 1984), p. 134.

45 James M. Washington, ed., *A Testament of Hope—The Essential Writings of Martin Luther King, Jr.* (San Francisco: Harper & Row Publishers, 1986), pp. 265-66.

46 Lawrence O. Richards, *A Theology of Christian Education* (Grand Rapids, MI: Zondervan Publishing House, 1975), p. 132.

47 Ibid., pp. 132-34.

48 William H. Myers, *God's Yes Was Louder Than My No—Rethinking the African American Call to Ministry* (Grand Rapids, MI: William B. Eerdmans Publishing Company, 1994), p. 2.

49 Gangel and Benson, p. 301.

50 Ibid., p. 300.

51 Knowles, *The Modern Practice of Adult Education*, pp. 18-19.

52 Ibid.

53 Knowles, *Self-Directed Learning*, pp. 31-34.

54 Lowell E. Brown and Bobbie Reed, *Your Sunday School Can Grow* (Glendale: Regal Books, 1974), p. 13.

55 Lawrence O. Richards, *A Theology of Children's Ministry* (Grand Rapids, MI: Zondervan Publishing House, 1983), p. 291.

56 Knowles, *Self-Directed Learning*, p. 60.

57 Linda J. Vogel, *Teaching Older Adults* (Nashville: Discipleship Resources, 1989), p. 21.

58 *Foundations*, p. 55.

59 Brown and Reed, p. 12.

60 Ibid., p. 14.

61 Anthony J. Shipley, "Choosing and Using Resources in the Black Church" (Nashville: The United Methodist Publishing House, Graded Press, 1973), p.1.

62 Ibid., pp.1-5.

63 Janice E. Hale-Benson, *Black Children—Their Roots, Culture, and Learning Styles* (Baltimore: The Johns Hopkins University Press, 1986), p. 154.

64 Ibid.

65 Ibid.

66 Paulo Freire, *Pedagogy of the Oppressed* (New York: Continuum Publishing Corporation, 1985), p. 69.

67 Hale-Benson, pp. 163-64.

68 Ibid., p. 165.

69 Williams, *God's Yes*, pp. 14-15.

70 Mary A. Love, "Musings on Sunday School in the Black Community," in *Renewing the Sunday School and the CCD,* ed. D. Campbell Wyckoff (Birmingham: Religious Education Press, 1986), pp. 162-66.

71 Richard B. Wilke, *Signs and Wonders—The Mighty Work of God in the Church* (Nashville: Abingdon Press, 1989), p. 14.

72 James S. Thomas, "Doctor of Ministry Regional Seminar Lecture," session conducted at United Theological Seminary, February 19-20, Dayton, Ohio.

73 Bennie E. Goodwin, II, *The Effective Teacher—A Christian's Guide to Teaching* (Downers Grove, IL: Intervarsity Press, 1985), p. 25.

74 Sid Smith, p 84.

75 Ibid., pp. 84-87.

76 Howard C. Hendricks, *Teaching to Change Lives* (Portland, OR: Multomah Press, 1987), p. 25.

77 Sid Smith, *10 Super Sunday Schools in the Black Community* (Nashville: Broadman Press, 1986), p. 105.

78 John H. Westerhoff, III, *Bringing Up Children in the Christian Faith* (Minneapolis: The Winston Press, 1980), pp. 36-37.

79 Richards, *A Theology of Christian Education,* p. 193.

80 Smith, *Reaching the Black Community Through the Sunday School,* pp. 144-46.

81 Brown and Reed, p. 28.

82 Ibid., p. 29.

83 Ibid., pp. 30-31.

84 Ibid., pp. 31-32.

85 Ibid., p. 33.

86 *Foundations for Teaching and Learning in The United Methodist Church* (Nashville: Discipleship Resources, 1979), p. 69.

87 Perry G. Downs, "Teaching Adults," in *The Christian Education of Adults,* ed. Gilbert A. Peterson (Chicago: Moody Press, 1984), p. 89.

88 Ibid., p. 90.

89 Ibid., pp. 91-93.

90 Norma J. Everist, *Education Ministry in the Congregation* (Minneapolis: Augsburg Publishing House, 1983), pp. 38-40.

91 Ibid., pp. 42-45.

92 Ibid.

93 Hendricks, p. 70.

94 John C. Elias, *The Foundations and Practice of Adult Religious Education* (Malabar, FL: Robert E. Krieger Publishing Company, 1982), pp. 253-54.

95 Paul Nichols, "Blacks and the Religious Education Movement," in *Changing Patterns of Religious Education,* ed. Marvin J. Taylor (Nashville: Abingdon Press, 1984), p. 181.

96 Love, p. 155.

97 "Black People and Their United Methodist Heritage," in *The Book of Discipline of The United Methodist Church* (Nashville: United Methodist Publishing House, 1976), pp. 14-15.

98 Frederick A. Norwood, *The Story of American Methodism* (Nashville: Abingdon Press, 1974), p. 58.

99 Ibid., p. 186.

100 William B. McClain, *Black People in the Methodist Church—Whither Thou Goest?* (Cambridge: Schenkman Publishing Company, 1984), p. 21.

101 Glenn C. Smith, ed., *Evangelizing Blacks* (Wheaton, IL: Tyndale House Publishers, Inc., 1988), p. 9.

102 Wallace Charles Smith, *The Church in the Life of the Black Family* (Valley Forge, PA: Judson Press, 1985), pp. 26-27.

103 Roy H. Ryan, *Invitational Teaching—Your Witness as a Sunday School Teacher* (Nashville: Discipleship Resources, 1988), pp. 7-8.

104 James O. Stallings, *Telling the Story—Evangelism in Black Churches* (Valley Forge, PA: Judson Press, 1988), pp. 118-19.

105 Smith, *Reaching the Black Community Through the Sunday School*, p. 141-42.

106 Vincie Alessi, *Evangelism in Your Church School* (Valley Forge, PA: Judson Press, 1978), p. 7.

107 McClain, p. 137.

108 Sid Smith, *Reaching the Black Community Through the Sunday School*, p. 139.

109 Ibid., p. 140.

110 Ibid., pp. 140-41.

111 Ibid., p. 141.

112 Ibid.

113 "Sunday School May Keep Kids Out of Jail, Study," *Jet*, December 22, 1986, p. 13.

114 "Return to Spiritual Traditions of Black Churches and School," *Ebony*, August 1986, p. 162.

115 William R. Johnson, "The Black Church and the Sunday School Movement," *The Church School Herald Journal 66*, no. 2 (December, January, February, 1980-81), p. 11.

116 John H. Westerhoff, III, *Living the Faith Community—The Church That Makes a Difference* (Minneapolis: Winston Press, Inc., 1985), p. 80.

117 Ibid.

118 Duane A. Ewers, *Do You Care? Compassion in the Sunday School* (Nashville: Discipleship Resources, 1988), pp. 8-17.

119 Ibid.

120 Carlyle Fielding Stewart III, *African American Church Growth—12 Principles for Prophetic Ministry* (Nashville: Abingdon Press, 1994), p. 89.

121 Ewers, *Do You Care?*, pp. 8-17.

122 Donald B. Rogers, *In Praise of Learning* (Nashville: Abingdon Press, 1980), p. 59.

123 Ewers, p. 10.

124 MaryJane Pierce Norton, *Teaching Young Children—A Guide for Teachers and Leaders* (Nashville: Discipleship Resources, 1989), p. 38.

125 Ewers, pp. 11-14.

126 Edward P. Wimberly, *Pastoral Counseling and Spiritual Values: A Black Point of View* (Nashville: Abingdon Press, 1982), pp. 141-42.

127 Ewers, pp. 16-17.

128 Ibid., p. 6.

129 Lois M. Runk, *Working with Elementary Children—A Guide for Teachers and Leaders* (Nashville: Discipleship Resources, 1988), p. 11.

130 Pierce Norton, p. 41.

131 Kennon L. Callahan, *Twelve Keys to an Effective Church* (San Francisco: Harper & Row Publishers, 1983), pp. 98-99.

132 Pillow and Youngblood, p. 17.

133 "Assessing Your Educational Ministry," in *Christian Education Planning Handbook*, ed. Roy H. Ryan (Nashville: Discipleship Resources, 1988), p. 5.

134 Felkner, p. 17.